What About Giants in the Bible?

Dear Lydia,
May God Bless You
And may you have
a Prosperous journey!
Annie & Marcia

ISBN: 0692810285
ISBN-13: 978-0692810286

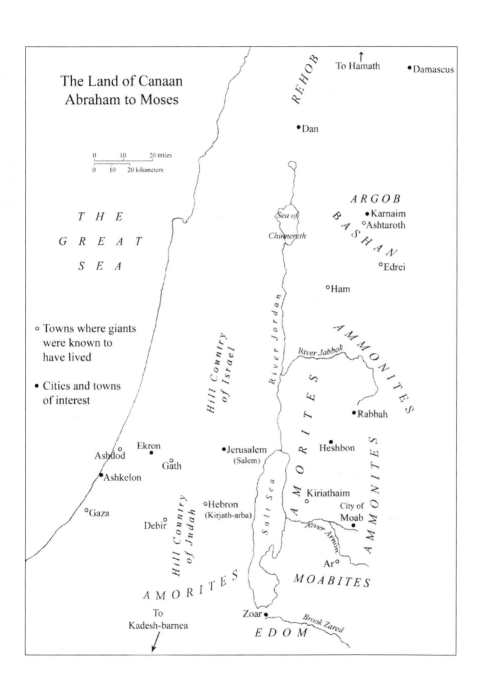

The Land of Canaan
Abraham to Moses

To Hamath

•Damascus

REHOB

•Dan

0   10   20 miles
0   10   20 kilometers

T H E

G R E A T

S E A

ARGOB

B A S H A N

Sea of

•Karnaim
°Ashtaroth

Chinnereth

°Edrei

°Ham

River Jordan

Hill Country of Israel

AMMONITES

River Jabbok

o Towns where giants
were known to
have lived

• Cities and towns
of interest

A M O R I T E S

•Rabbah

Ekron
Ashdod °
•
Gath °

•Jerusalem
(Salem)

Heshbon
°

AMMONITES

•Ashkelon

°Gaza

Debir °

°Hebron
(Kirjath-arba)

Salt Sea

A M O R I T E S

Kiriathaim
°

City of
Moab •

River Arnon

A M M O N I T E S

Hill Country of Judah

A M O R I T E S

Ar°

MOABITES

To
Kadesh-barnea

Zoar •

Brook Zared

E D O M

WHAT ABOUT GIANTS IN THE BIBLE?

Table of Contents

Preface

God bless you in the wonderful name of Jesus Christ, and thank you for reading *What About Giants in the Bible?*

First of all, I believe the Bible is true. I believe it contains the words of God and that they are truth. This was so pointedly stated by Jesus Christ in the Gospel of John, in his magnificent prayer to God shortly before his sacrifice for all mankind.

> John 17:17
> Sanctify them through thy truth: thy word is truth.

For many today it is not in vogue to believe the Scriptures are true. However, I would rather be in agreement with Jesus Christ's opinion in these regards rather than with some intellectuals of today who disagree.

Initially, I did not start out to write a book considering what the Bible has to say about giants. I had been working on a project for a number of years when I came to Genesis chapter 6. Verses 1-8 of this chapter address life on earth before the Flood that happened in the days of Noah. From a careful consideration of Genesis chapter 5, one can determine that there was a time period of 1,656 years from the creation of Adam until the Flood. This is a very long period of time about which to have such limited information available. However, one can glean a great deal of information from just a few verses of God's Word. This

i

particular section of Scripture in Genesis chapter 6 mentions giants living on the earth, "in those days and also after that." I was intrigued.

This book started off as an endeavor to see and understand more of what God's Word has to say about giants in the Bible. At first this was going to be included as an appendix to the project I was working on at the time. But the more I learned and the more detailed my study of this subject became, it became evident to my family, friends, and finally myself that this should be considered worthy of standing on its own.

I did not start out with a preset position I wanted to present or expound upon. I started out with questions. I have endeavored to present this topic in the same manner which I approached it, and with the same question: what about giants in the Bible?

I began with an outline of questions I wanted to find answers to, the same ones presented as chapters in this book. My aim was to discover, and later on to present, what the Bible has to say about giants.

In addition to the primary consideration of discovering what the Bible has to say about giants, there are also several appendices to aid in this study. The first is a map of the Bible lands with towns and landmarks of interest to help picture the locations of which the Scriptures speak.

There is also a size comparison chart to illustrate the differences between the size of the giants and the men who encountered them.

Next, there is an appendix considering the conception of Jesus Christ. This is included because of questions which arose regarding humans and spirit beings cohabiting.

Finally, an appendix listing articles from the New York Times related to archeological discoveries of giant skeletons is included.

What I have learned has been thrilling and exciting to me, and it is my hope that it will be to you also.

Donnie Lamb, June 2015.

Acknowledgements

I wish to give my sincere thanks to everyone who has helped me with this endeavor. Quite honestly, "thanks" is not a strong enough word for how much I appreciate all the kind words, questions, ideas, encouragement, and help with the English language. There have been many, many times during the editing phase of this project that I have felt that English is for me a second language. The embarrassing thing is, it's the only language I speak.

First I must thank my wonderful wife Marcia, who puts up with me and loves me despite all my short comings. Her encouragement has been paramount in this endeavor ever being carried through to completion.

Next, to my daughter-in-law Angela and daughter Carli: this would never have happened without your help with grammar, editing, and formatting (not like this is a revelation to them). Without your help this project would not even have been worthy of being a coloring book. Thanks also to Phil, Aaron, Murphy, and Joe. I have the most wonderful and talented family a man could ever desire.

And thanks to all of the local believers of the Spokane, Washington area who have been so gracious in listening to me talk incessantly about this project as it developed.

To everyone whose questions, comments, and suggestions have been so helpful, thank you, too. You all know who you are, and so does our Heavenly Father.

Lastly, and most importantly, to our Heavenly Father Who included this information in His wonderful Word: thank You for including it and so much more.

Romans 15:4
For whatsoever things were written aforetime were written for our learning, that we through patience and comfort of the scriptures might have hope.

Introduction

Before considering this study on giants in the Bible, it is of great importance to first consider the words of II Peter 1:20 and 21.

> II Peter 1:20-21
> Knowing this first, that no prophecy of the scripture is of any private interpretation.
>
> For the prophecy came not in old time by the will of man: but holy men of God spake as they were moved by the Holy Ghost.

The Bible says of itself that it is not intended for private, or one's own, interpretation. The reason for this is given in the following verse: because the words did not come by the will of man. The words came as holy men of God spoke as they were moved by the Holy Ghost, meaning the Holy Spirit, God. This is why it is not intended for one's own interpretation. The Scriptures are words from God. They carry His intended meaning. These verses also lead one to understand that although the Bible had many writers, there is only one Author, God. Not adhering to the instruction of II Peter 1:20 and 21 has resulted in numerous denominations in the Christian church today.

Logically thinking, if the Bible is not intended for one to privately interpret, then one is left with only two possibilities. Either it is not possible for the Bible to be understood, or it must interpret itself. The latter is exactly what it does. It does this primarily in three ways. It is either plain or clear right where it is written in the verse, or in the context of the verse, or it has explained itself previously. This was an epiphany to me when I first took a class about the Bible in 1975 which explained and taught these keys and others to understanding how God's Word interprets itself.

There are also additional keys to understanding how God's Word interprets itself. Utilizing these keys helps one greatly in becoming a workman of God's Word. For anyone interested in learning more about these keys and how God's Word interprets itself, I would be very happy to recommend a class which makes this knowledge available.

> II Timothy 2:15
> Study to shew thyself approved unto God, a workman that needeth not to be ashamed, rightly dividing the word of truth.

As a workman of God's Word, Timothy was encouraged to diligently study to present himself approved unto God, an unashamed worker, by rightly dividing the Word of truth.

It has been the goal of this project to search the Scriptures and to say what the Scriptures say without any private interpretation in order to see what God's Word has to say about giants in the Bible.

Part 1
What About Giants in the Bible?

When one reads of there being giants in the Bible, at first it seems preposterous and even akin to mythological tales. However, unlike mythological tales, God's Word is truth.[1] Therefore, what one reads concerning giants in the Bible is historical truth that God included for our learning, as holy men of God spoke and wrote as they were moved by the Holy Spirit, who is God.

When the spies sent out by Moses into the Promised Land came back reporting that there were giants in the land, men of such stature that the spies said of themselves they were as grasshoppers in their sight, they were not reproved for saying that giants existed. They, except for Joshua and Caleb, were reproved for their fear and lack of believing that God could deliver them into the land promised, despite men of such gigantic stature.

The first reference in the Bible to giants is in Genesis chapter 6.

> Genesis 6:4
> There were giants in the earth in those days; and also after that, when the sons of God came in unto the daughters of men, and they bare *children* to

---

[1] See John 17:17. For additional verses on this topic, see Ephesians 1:13, Colossians 1:5, I Thessalonians 2:13, I Timothy 2:4, John 14:6, II Timothy 2:15, and James 1:18.

1

them, the same *became* mighty men which *were* of old, men of renown.

In this first reference to there being giants in, or on, the earth, verse 4 includes a time reference with the phrase, "in those days." The days being referred to are the days and time before the Flood. But it also says, "and also after that," which would refer to the days and time after the Flood. This verse is the only verse in the Bible that specifically refers to there being giants before the Flood.

The Hebrew word used for giants here is the word *nephil,* which according to *Strong's Exhaustive Concordance of The Bible* is word H5303 and means, "properly, a *feller,* that is, a *bully* or *tyrant:* - giant." This definition certainly agrees with the context of Genesis chapter 6.

> Genesis 6:1-7
> And it came to pass, when men began to multiply on the face of the earth, and daughters were born unto them,
>
> That the sons of God saw the daughters of men that they *were* fair; and they took them wives of all which they chose.
>
> And the LORD said, My spirit shall not always strive with man, for that he also *is* flesh: yet his days shall be an hundred and twenty years.
>
> There were giants in the earth in those days; and also after that, when the sons of God came in unto the daughters of men, and they bare *children* to

them, the same *became* mighty men which *were* of old, men of renown.

And GOD saw that the wickedness of man *was* great in the earth, and *that* every imagination of the thoughts of his heart *was* only evil continually.

And it repented the LORD that he had made man on the earth, and it grieved him at his heart.

And the LORD said, I will destroy man whom I have created from the face of the earth; both man, and beast, and the creeping thing, and the fowls of the air; for it repenteth me that I have made them.

The context, specifically from Genesis 6:5, indicates that all of mankind was exceptionally wicked and evil to the extent that every intention of the thoughts and imaginations of his heart was evil continually. The men referred to as giants in Genesis 6:4 would not have been an exception and were men who were, no doubt, extremely wicked and evil, in addition to being defined by the word *nephil* as bullies and tyrants.

There are some who argue that the giants living before the Flood, referred to in Genesis 6:4, were giants of evil and wickedness only and were not men of gigantic stature. Although there are no other verses which speak directly of giants before the Flood, there is a verse in Numbers which gives one a more complete understanding of the word *nephil*. Interestingly, there are only three occurrences of the word *nephil* in the Bible; the first is in Genesis 6:4, and the other two are in Numbers 13:33.

Numbers 13:33
And there we saw the giants [*nephil*], the sons of Anak, *which come* of the giants [*nephil*]: and we were in our own sight as grasshoppers, and so we were in their sight.

The *nephil* were evidently so large that the children of Israel felt "as grasshoppers" in comparison. The *nephil* were tyrants and bullies, men of wickedness and evil, in addition to being men of gigantic physical stature. Genesis 6:4 also says, "the same *became* mighty men which *were* of old, men of renown." They were men of renown, men of fame exalted by not only their reputation of wickedness and evil but also by their gigantic stature. They were tyrants and bullied the people by means of their great evil, wickedness, and size, which, before the Flood, further contributed to the wickedness of all mankind.

Since there is only one reference to there being giants before the Flood, it is difficult to search out any more verses for information concerning them. After the Flood is a different matter. There are numerous verses in the Scriptures that provide details about giants that lived after the Flood.

This consideration of giants in the Bible is by no means an exhaustive study on the subject but an overview of information provided from selected verses concerning them. In this consideration we will examine:

- How did the giants originate?
- Who were the giants? When and where did they live?
- How large were the giants?
- What happened to the giants?

Part 2
How Did the Giants Originate?

Since the Bible speaks of there having been giants both before and after the Flood, this leads one to wonder **how** they originated. Rather than joining in with the speculation of some and the wild theories that seem to abound, let's take the time to consider what God's Word has to say about how giants originated, and how it fits with science as well. We will begin by examining how the giants did *not* originate.

Chapter 2.1
How the Giants Did Not Originate

In this consideration of giants in the Bible, it is first needful to consider how the giants did **not** originate. This is necessary because some have postulated the theory that the giants spoken of in the Bible were the result of spirit beings mating with human females. This speculation is primarily due to misunderstanding and misapplying the phrase "sons of God" found in Genesis 6:2 and 4, and Job 1:6. These three verses are listed below.

> Genesis 6:2
> That the **sons of God** [emphasis added] saw the daughters of men that they *were* fair; and they took them wives of all which they chose.

> Genesis 6:4
> There were giants in the earth in those days; and also after that, when the **sons of God** [emphasis added] came in unto the daughters of men, and they bare *children* to them, the same *became* mighty men which *were* of old, men of renown.

> Job 1:6
> Now there was a day when the **sons of God** [emphasis added] came to present themselves before the LORD, and Satan came also among them.

8

In order to rightly divide God's Word and arrive at the proper understanding, we, as students of God's Word, need to handle the Word of God honestly and without private interpretation in order to allow God's Word to speak for itself. If there are any difficult verses, we need to handle those in light of the clear ones on the same topic because God's Word must fit together without contradictions.

The phrase "sons of God" from Genesis 6:2 and 4 has caused difficulty for many, especially when read in conjunction with Job 1:6. It has been assumed by some that the phrase "sons of God" in Genesis 6:2 and 4 is referring to angels or some type of spirit being because it is referring to angels in Job 1:6.

Angels are created spirit beings. There is no biblical evidence that angels, or spirit beings of any category, can reproduce. Spirit beings can no more reproduce offspring with human beings than human beings can reproduce offspring with plant life. In each of these: spirit life, soul life, and plant life, there is life, but they are not compatible life forms to reproduce with one another. God's Word explains in Genesis chapter 1 that everything that reproduces does so "after his kind."

> Genesis 1:11-12
> And God said, Let the earth bring forth grass, the herb yielding seed, *and* the fruit tree yielding fruit after his kind, whose seed *is* in itself, upon the earth: and it was so.

9

And the earth brought forth grass, *and* herb yielding seed after his kind, and the tree yielding fruit, whose seed *was* in itself, after his kind: and God saw that *it was* good.

All plant life reproduces via seed within itself and after its kind. This is a foundational law of genetic reproduction and also applies to beings with soul life, as explained beginning in verse 21 of the same chapter.

Genesis 1:21
And God created great whales, and every living creature that moveth, which the waters brought forth abundantly, after their kind, and every winged fowl after his kind: and God saw that *it was* good.

The word "creature" in verse 21 is the Hebrew word *nephesh*, meaning soul; soul life.[2] Soul life is breath life and is contained in the blood, as explained from Leviticus 17:11: "For the life of the flesh *is* in the blood."

Genesis 1:24-25
And God said, Let the earth bring forth the living creature [*nephesh*, soul] after his kind, cattle, and creeping thing, and beast of the earth after his kind: and it was so.

And God made the beast of the earth after his kind, and cattle after their kind, and every thing that

---

[2] *Strong's Exhaustive Concordance of the Bible,* word # H5315

creepeth upon the earth after his kind: and God saw that *it was* good.

So far, God's Word has explained that all life on the earth reproduces "after his kind" from seed within itself. This is true for plants as well as all soul life. For soul life, it requires the joining of the male and female of the species in order for the seed to fertilize the egg. Soul life is the type of life which animates all fish, birds, as well as all living creatures upon the earth. This also includes mankind.

> Genesis 2:7
> And the LORD God formed man *of* the dust of the ground, and breathed into his nostrils the breath of life; and man became a living soul [*nephesh*].

God's Word pointedly shows that all plant life and soul life reproduce after their kind from seed contained within. This is a foundational law of genetic reproduction.

Let's think logically for a moment. If spirit life could produce offspring with soul life, why would it have only happened before the Flood and again shortly thereafter? What would stop this from continuing to happen right up to this present time? There is no biblical or biological evidence of this ever happening. This would violate the foundational laws of genetic reproduction, which are explained in the first chapter of Genesis.

There is a legitimate explanation for the phrase "sons of God" used in Genesis 6:2 and 4, and Job 1:6; it is a figure of speech known as a Hebraism, an idiom from the Hebrew language.

Figures of speech in the Bible are used by God to call attention and to add emphasis. The phrase "sons of God" is used in these verses as a figure of speech. Figures of speech do not weaken the words of God, but rather they strengthen them by providing emphasis. When something is said in God's Word and it is not true in a literal sense, or the grammatical structure deviates from correct form, then it is a figure of speech.[3]

It bears pointing out the phrase "sons of God" can also be used literally **without** it being a figure of speech, as it is used in various verses found in the New Testament. Since the original outpouring of holy spirit recorded in Acts chapter 2, it has been available for an individual who confesses Jesus as Lord and believes God raised him from the dead to become born again, born from above.[4] In so doing, this makes that individual a son of God.

> I John 3:1 and 2
> Behold, what manner of love the Father hath bestowed upon us, that we should be called the **sons of God** [emphasis added]: therefore the world knoweth us not, because it knew him not.

---

[3] E.W. Bullinger, *Figures of Speech Used In The Bible,* Reprinted 1968 by Baker Book House Company, pages iii – xv.

[4] Romans 10:9,10: That if thou shalt confess with thy mouth the Lord Jesus, and shalt believe in thine heart that God hath raised him from the dead, thou shalt be saved. For with the heart man believeth unto righteousness; and with the mouth confession is made unto salvation.

Beloved, now are we the **sons of God** [emphasis added], and it doth not yet appear what we shall be: but we know that, when he shall appear, we shall be like him; for we shall see him as he is.

Being a son of God by having been born again, born from above, was not available before the original outpouring of spirit as recorded in Acts chapter 2. That is when it first became available to become a son of God. This is what arrests one's attention in Genesis 6:2 and 4, and in Job 1:6 with the phrase "sons of God." It is a figure of speech calling one's attention to this because it is not true in a literal sense.

In different languages, there exist numerous idiomatic terms that do not translate, or translate fully, to other languages. A Hebraism is one such example. A Hebraism describes numerous idiomatic words or phrases used by the Hebrew people that have a deeper, or fuller, meaning in their language than the words represent in other languages.

A modern day example of an idiomatic term in our language could be "band of brothers." Just as the Hebrew idiom "sons of God" conveyed a deeper, or fuller meaning to them, "band of brothers" does to many of us. We know a band of brothers typically is not referring to a musical group of male siblings. The deeper, or fuller, meaning is a group of soldiers who have trained together, depended upon one another, and have been bonded together by the hardship of war. They are as close, or closer, to one another as sibling brothers could be. One could simply say "a company of soldiers" but it would not convey the deeper meaning as the idiom "band of brothers" does.

If someone were to say, "Don't put God's Word on the back burner," we as English speakers would realize he or she didn't literally mean not to put the Bible on the stove. This phrase would communicate to us not to put the Bible in a position of less importance than something else, or not to procrastinate on reading it or doing what it says. While we know what this idiomatic phrase means, using it gives the phrase more emphasis, because it causes us to stop and consider that it isn't literally true, and then to consider what the phrase really means. Our minds pause and reflect for a split second longer than if someone simply says, "Don't put God's Word in a position of less importance."

There are many other examples of idioms in our language such as "cover your bases," "feel like a million bucks," and "spill the beans," just to name a few. These phrases are difficult for many non-native English speakers to understand because they aren't literally true when translated into their native language.

Webster's Dictionary of 1828 has the following explanation for the word "son" under usage number 9: "9. Son of pride, sons of light, son of Belial. These are Hebraisms, which denote that persons possess the qualities of pride, of light, or of Belial, as children inherit the qualities of their ancestors." [5]

In Genesis chapter 6 verses 2 and 4 "sons of God" is used as a Hebraism, meaning men who inherited, or manifested, the qualities of those who follow after God. Those primarily would be qualities such as believing God and doing His Will. The "sons of God" spoken of are put in opposition to the "daughters of men," who did not follow the will of God, but rather their own will.

The same is true in Job 1:6. "Sons of God" is used in this context also as a Hebraism, speaking of the angels of God who manifested the qualities of being faithful to and following after God rather than rebelling and following after Satan. They were not "sons of God" in a literal sense. The point of the idiom "sons of God" being used in this verse is to illustrate how dissident it was for Satan to present himself before God with the angels who had remained faithful to God.

> Genesis 6:1-2
> And it came to pass, when men began to multiply on the face of the earth, and daughters were born unto them,
>
> That the sons of God saw the daughters of men that they *were* fair; and they took them wives of all which they chose.

---

[5] Webster's Dictionary 1828 - Online Edition, "Son", 2016-11-14, http://webstersdictionary1828.com/Dictionary/son

Genesis 6:1 is speaking of when **men** began multiplying on the face of the earth, not spirit beings. Verse 2 refers to some of these men as "sons of God"—men who manifested the qualities of those who follow after God. Before the Flood, there were men who endeavored to follow after God, and there were men who did not, which was exemplified by the lives of Cain and Abel recorded in Genesis chapter 4. The "daughters of men" is referring to women who did not follow after God, but rather their own will. The men who followed after God saw that the daughters of men, who did not follow after God, were fair. They considered them very attractive, so they took the daughters of men to be their wives. The results of this were catastrophic and are related in the following verses.

> Genesis 6:3-7
> And the LORD said, My spirit shall not always strive with man, for that he also *is* flesh: yet his days shall be an hundred and twenty years.[6]

---

[6] There are some who believe this verse is referring to the first man Adam because the Hebrew word used for man in this verse is *adam*. However, this cannot be referring to the first man Adam for two reasons: the first is context, and the second is that by the time of the Flood Adam had been dead for 726 years.

The context of Genesis chapter 6 is stated in the opening verse as, "And it came to pass when men began to multiply on the face of the earth and daughters were born unto them." The chapter then moves on into details of the degradation of mankind and verse 2 begins an explanation of how this happened. This context begins in verse 1 and continues through verse 8. Verse 9 begins a new topic. To say that verse 3 is talking about the original man Adam does not fit within this context.

There were giants in the earth in those days; and also after that, when the sons of God came in unto the daughters of men, and they bare *children* to them, the same *became* mighty men which *were* of old, men of renown.

And GOD saw that the wickedness of man *was* great in the earth, and *that* every imagination of the thoughts of his heart *was* only evil continually.

And it repented the LORD that he had made man on the earth, and it grieved him at his heart.

And the LORD said, I will destroy man whom I have created from the face of the earth; both man, and beast, and the creeping thing, and the fowls of the air; for it repenteth me that I have made them.

The end result of the men who followed after God marrying the daughters of men, who did not follow after God, was indeed tragically catastrophic because the daughters of men influenced the sons of God so adversely that even they became like everyone else referred to in Genesis 6:5.

He has not been the subject of the context since the conclusion of chapter 3.

Adam lived a total of 930 years. Noah was born 126 years after Adam died. The Flood began in the 600th year of Noah's life. This means Adam would have been dead for 726 years when the Flood began. The "hundred and twenty years" referred to in verse 3 of chapter 6 cannot be referring to the last 120 years of the patriarch Adam's life but rather is referring to mankind in general. The Hebrew word *adam* is also used extensively as a pronoun referring to mankind in general, a human being. See *Strong's Analytical concordance to the Bible*, word H120.

Genesis 6:5-6

And GOD saw that the wickedness of man *was* great in the earth, and *that* every imagination of the thoughts of his heart *was* only evil continually.

And it repented the LORD that he had made man on the earth, and it grieved him at his heart.

The phrases "sons of God" and "daughters of men" are not referring to spirit beings having sexual relations with human beings. Understanding the Hebrew idiom being utilized and reading in context Genesis chapter 6, verses 1 through 6, along with the larger context of chapters 4 and 5, one can understand it is an explanation about the condition of mankind as mankind grew and multiplied on the face of the earth before the Flood. It is an explanation of how mankind became the way it did. How sad a commentary that mankind turned out to be so wicked and evil that it repented the Lord that He had made man, and it grieved Him in His heart.

Chapter 2.2
How the Giants Did Originate

We have considered how the giants **did not** originate from spirit beings mating with human females and producing offspring. Next we will look at how the giants **did** originate.

Verse 4 of Genesis chapter 6 tells us that when the sons of God came in unto the daughters of men, children were born unto them.

> Genesis 6:4
> There were giants in the earth in those days; and also after that, **when the sons of God came in unto the daughters of men, and they bare *children* to them,** [emphasis added] the same *became* mighty men which *were* of old, men of renown.

The honest answer to what produced the giants before the Flood is the same answer as what produced the giants after the Flood: genetics.

Today, there is no race of giants. There, however, isolated examples of the medical condition known as giantism, which is very rare. Giantism is a medical condition caused by the pituitary gland secreting too much growth hormone, leading to changes in the normal growth of the body.[7] This medical condition is also known as acromegaly in adults. Acromegaly, caused by a tumor on

---

[7] http://pituitary.ucla.edu/resources

the pituitary gland, can produce a wide array of symptoms. Many times these symptoms include abnormal enlargement of the hands and feet, enlargement of the forehead and jaw, and a deepening of the voice in males. Left untreated, excessive asymmetrical growth of the body and deformities can also occur. The sufferers can sometimes exhibit extreme feebleness and difficulty in even walking.

Many people are familiar with some modern cases of acromegaly, including André René Roussimoff, better known as André the Giant, who reached a height of seven feet and four inches and manifested many of these symptoms.

The tallest person in modern history was Robert Wadlow (February 22, 1918 – July 15, 1940). Mr. Wadlow suffered from acromegaly caused by a tumor on his pituitary gland and was 8 feet 11 inches tall. His growth was somewhat asymmetrical and he experienced various health problems in addition to experiencing difficulty in walking. He only lived to be 22 years old.

However, in some cases giantism is not caused by a tumor on the pituitary gland but is caused by a mutated gene and can be passed on genetically.[8] The observation that living things inherit traits from their parents has been understood throughout history. This was described in detail by Gregor Mendel in his laws of genetics. Mendel's laws deal with the

---

[8]"In a Giant's Story, a New Chapter Writ by His DNA" by Gina Kolata. The New York Times, January 5, 2011.

combination of dominant and recessive genetic traits and the results of these combinations.

Speculation and theories must not be taken as truths until proven. Mendel's laws are so proven they are called and correctly applied as laws.

The DNA sequence of a gene varies from one individual to another. These variations are called alleles. Most genes have two or more alleles. One allele is inherited from the male parent and one from the female parent. The degree of similarity of the alleles for a trait in an organism is called zygosity.

When genes have identical alleles from both parents they are said to be homozygous. An individual that is homozygous-dominant for a particular trait carries two copies of the allele that code for the dominant trait. An individual that is homozygous-recessive for a particular trait carries two copies of the allele that code for the recessive trait.[9]

Inbreeding is the mating of closely related individuals, such as cousins or siblings, which increases the number of individuals in the gene pool that are homozygous for a trait

---

[9] Carr, M; Cotton, S.; Rogers, D.; Pomiankowski, A.; Smith, H.; Fowler, K. (2006) "Assigning sex to pre-adult stalk-eyed flies using genetic disc morphology and X chromosome zygosity". BMC developmental biology 6: 29 doi: 10.1186/1471-213X-6-29.

and can produce a particular genetic strain or mutation.[10] Inbreeding does not always produce harmful traits. For instance, inbreeding in livestock is a technique used to try to establish a new or desirable trait in that stock. However, with livestock, harmful and undesirable traits can be culled, something not morally or ethically possible with humans.

The expected percentage of homozygosity arising from inbreeding was defined mathematically by Sewall Wright in his paper "Coefficients of inbreeding and relationship", published in 1922.[11] The coefficient of inbreeding can be used to express degrees of kinship in numeric terms in human genealogy resulting in offspring with two dominant or two recessive alleles, and describes how many genes would be expected to be matching between the two people. Some percentages for the amount of matching genes between combinations of related people are as follows:

Relationship	
identical twins/clones	100%
parent-offspring	50%
full siblings	50%
half siblings	25%
double first cousins (share the same grandparents)	25%
first cousins	12.5%
second cousins	3.13%

---

[10] Livingston, F.B. (1969) "Genetics, Ecology, and the Origins of Incest and Exogamy". Current Anthropology 10: 45-62. doi: 10. 1086/201009.

[11] Wright, Sewall (1922). "Coefficients of inbreeding and relationship". *American Naturalist* 56:3330-338. Doi:10 1086/279872.

The study of genetics shows that when small family groups only breed among themselves, specific genetic characteristics will arise very quickly.[12] There are three examples of this happening early on in human history in the book of Genesis. The first was before the Flood when the sons and daughters of Adam and Eve began to multiply. Initially, there was no one else for them to marry other than their own brothers and sisters. Even the next generation could only have mated with double first cousins at best. As the sons and daughters of Adam and Eve and their offspring could only breed among themselves, the laws of genetics dictate that distinctive genetic traits would have begun to manifest very rapidly.

The next example of small family groups breeding only among themselves was as a result of the Flood, which left only six people for breeding and repopulating the earth: the three sons of Noah and their wives.[13] Once again, these six individuals and their offspring could only breed among themselves, and this would have resulted in distinctive genetic traits being manifested.

The third example was a result of the language dispersion that occurred at Babel. As family groups became isolated by language barriers and only bred among themselves, once

---

[12] Tim Osterholm, "The Table of Nations (Genealogy of Mankind) and the Origin of Races (History of Man)", 10-15-2016, http://www.soundchristian.com/man.

[13] There is no record of Noah and his wife producing any other offspring before or after the Flood other than their 3 sons.

again according to the laws of genetics, distinguishing genetic traits would have begun to appear very rapidly.[14]

The repeated mating of closely related individuals that occurred on these three occasions explains why the giants spoken of in the Bible were manifested when they were— before the Flood and very quickly again following the Flood.

Geneticists have proven that the isolation of breeding groups that only breed among themselves can result in the formation of different races, as the matching alleles combine to produce the same traits over and over, further distinguishing the offspring. Fixation of alleles can occur when a population's genomes accumulate mutations that are irreversible.[15,16]

One can see the results of this today with the different races of mankind. There are three distinct families from which the characteristics of mankind after the Flood originated. These three families make the oldest table of nations in existence. The three families are from the three sons of Noah: Shem, Ham, and Japheth. This is how the present world population originated and spread after the Flood,

---

[14] Tim Osterholm, "The Table of Nations (Genealogy of Mankind) and the Origin of Races (History of Man)", 10-15-2016, http://www.soundchristian.com/man.

[15] Hartl, D.L., Jones E.W. (2000) "Genetics: analysis of Genes and Genomes". Fifth Edition. Jones and Bartlett Publishers Inc. pp 105-106. ISBN 0763715115.

[16] Leek, Charles F. (1980) "Establishment of New Population Centers With Changes in Migration Patterns". (PDF) Journal of Field Ornithology 51 (2): 168-173.

which is recorded in Genesis chapter 10. Here, one can learn the true divisions of mankind, indicating how the present population of the world came to be.[17]

Race, however, does not apply to skin color alone. Race is a classification system used to categorize humans into large and distinct populations or groups by anatomical, cultural, ethnic, genetic, geographical, historical, linguistic, religious, and/or social affiliation.[18] Just as family groups began to repeatedly manifest different skin color traits and facial features, there was a group, or groups, which, due to breeding within family groups, developed a mutated gene and began to genetically manifest gigantic size among their community. This is how the giants originated. As they continued to breed among themselves, families grew into tribes and tribes of giants grew into a race of giants. This race of giants can biblically be traced back to their tribes and even, in one instance, back to their originating family.

---

[17] Tim Osterholm, "The Table of Nations (Genealogy of Mankind) and the Origin of Races (History of Man)", 10-15-2016, http://www.soundchristian.com/man.
[18] Definition of race – "ethnic group, anthropology, personal attribute." *Oxford Dictionaries*. Oxford University Press. Retrieved 5 October 2014.

Part 3
Who Were the Giants?
When and Where Did They Live?

We have considered how the giants recorded in the Bible did not originate and how they did originate. Next we will look at records from the Scriptures regarding who the giants were, and we will also consider when and where they lived.

Chapter 3.1
Giants in the Days of Moses

One time period in which giants lived, according to the Scriptures, is during the lifetime of Moses.

The Anakims

The first group of giants we will encounter during the time of Moses is the Anakims, or the sons of Anak.

After leaving Egypt, and **before** spending 40 years in the wilderness, God had the children of Israel camped in Kadesh-barnea, poised to enter into the Promised Land (See Appendix 1). There, at God's instruction, Moses sent one man from each tribe of Israel (12 in all) to search and spy out the land prior to the entire nation entering into the land to possess it.

The spies started from Kadesh-barnea and entered the land from the south. From this exploration, they returned with reports of there being giants in the land.

> Numbers 13:17-22
> And Moses sent them to spy out the land of Canaan, and said unto them, Get you up this *way* southward, and go up into the mountain:
>
> And see the land, what it *is;* and the people that dwelleth therein, whether they *be* strong or weak, few or many;

And what the land *is* that they dwell in, whether it *be* good or bad; and what cities *they be* that they dwell in, whether in tents, or in strong holds;

And what the land *is,* whether it *be* fat or lean, whether there be wood therein, or not. And be ye of good courage, and bring of the fruit of the land. Now the time *was* the time of the firstripe grapes.

So they went up, and searched the land from the wilderness of Zin unto Rehob, as men come to Hamath.

And they ascended by the south, and came unto Hebron; where Ahiman, Sheshai, and Talmai, the children of Anak, *were.* (Now Hebron was built seven years before Zoan in Egypt.)

As the spies traveled up from the south, they came to Hebron, where Ahiman, Sheshai, and Talmai, the children of Anak, were. These were the giants that the spies brought news of when they returned back to Moses, and in verse 22 they were referred to as "the children of Anak."

Numbers 13:32-33
And they [the spies except Joshua and Caleb] brought up an evil report of the land which they had searched unto the children of Israel, saying, The land, through which we have gone to search it, *is* a land that eateth up the inhabitants thereof; and all the people that we saw in it *are* men of a great stature.

> And there we saw the giants [*nephil*], the sons of Anak, *which come* of the giants [*nephil*]: and we were in our own sight as grasshoppers, and so we were in their sight.

From the spies' comments upon their return, one could reason that they must have had some type of contact and dialog beyond observation from afar. Otherwise, how would the spies have known the names of the giants and that the giants looked upon the spies as they themselves also felt—as grasshoppers?

This was a major turning point for the nation of Israel. They once again rebelled against God, refusing to enter the land He had promised to their fathers. One of the reasons listed for their refusal to enter into the land was that the land was inhabited by giants. In Numbers 13:33 these giants are called "the sons of Anak." "Sons of Anak" is a Hebrasiam[19] referring to the qualities that the descendants of Anak inherited and manifested. From this context it would mean they were men of gigantic size. From our previous consideration of the Hebrew word *nephil*, it would also mean they were tyrants and bullies.

Since these "sons of Anak" were so emphatically reported of by the spies and had such an impact on them, let's consider what else the Scriptures reveal about this group.

---

[19] *Webster's Dictionary*; son; usage 9. "Son of pride, sons of light, son of Belial. These are Hebraisms, which denote that persons possess the qualities of pride, of light, or of Belial, as children inherit the qualities of their ancestors."

There is not an abundance of information recorded in the Bible concerning Anak. However, one can gain additional insight concerning him and his family from reading a passage about when Caleb was given his inheritance in the Promised Land over 40 years later.

> Joshua 15:13
> And unto Caleb the son of Jephunneh he gave a part among the children of Judah, according to the commandment of the LORD to Joshua, *even* the city of Arba the father of Anak, which *city is* Hebron.

According to this verse, Hebron was the city of Arba, and Arba was the father of Anak. Judges 1:10 gives additional information about the city of Hebron.

> Judges 1:10
> And Judah went against the Canaanites that dwelt in Hebron: (now the name of Hebron before *was* Kirjatharba:)

Kirjatharba in Hebrew means "city of Arba". Prior to being known as Hebron, it was known as the city of Arba. This is confirmed in Joshua 14:15.

> Joshua 14:15a
> And the name of Hebron before *was* Kirjatharba; *which Arba was* a great man among the Anakims....

From these verses one can understand that Anak, the "father" of the Anakims, was the son of Arba, who himself was a great man among the Anakims. In addition, Kirjatharba, which was later known of as Hebron, was named after him. We have already read in Numbers 13:22 that the city of Hebron (where Sheshai, Ahiman, and Talmai, the sons of Anak, lived) was an old city built seven years before Zoan in Egypt.

It is difficult to date the founding of Kirjatharba (Hebron), but being founded seven years before Zoan[20] does give one a time reference.

Zoan was the capital of the early Egyptian Hyksos Dynasty also known as the Dynasty of the "Shepherd Kings." Its founding is believed to pre-date the time of Abraham.[21]

Although it is difficult to determine the exact founding of Kirjatharba, we can determine that by the days of Abraham it was already an established city. This is possible due to a verse in Genesis chapter 23 which states that Sarah, the beloved wife of Abraham, died there.

---

[20] Zoan, in *Young's Analytical Concordance to the Bible,* is referenced as the Hebrew word H6814 and spelled *Tso'an.* It is identified as an Egyptian city. "In Psalm 78, verses 12 and 43, Zoan is mentioned as "the field of Zoan" where Moses performed miracles before Pharaoh to persuade him to release Israel from his service. Zoan is also mentioned in Isaiah 19 verses 11, and 13, and in Isaiah 30:4; also in Ezekiel 30:14. In all of these verses Zoan is referred to in the Greek Septuagint by the Greek name *Tanis.*

[21] Smith, William, Dr., Entry for "Zoan", Smith's Bible Dictionary, 1901.

Orr, James, M.A., General Editor. Entry for "Zoan". International Standard Bible Encyclopedia". 1915.

Genesis 23:2
And Sarah died in Kirjatharba; the same *is* Hebron in the land of Canaan: and Abraham came to mourn for Sarah, and to weep for her.

This helps one to understand the antiquity of the city of Arba, also known as Hebron, and the Anakims, who were descendants of Anak, the son of Arba. The timing of their appearance would have been sometime after the Flood and before the time of Abraham. The Anakims were the first giants encountered by the children of Israel when the spies were sent out by Moses.

Og the King of Bashan

There is another giant which Moses and the children of Israel encountered as they journeyed to the Promised Land nearing the end of the 40 years spent in the wilderness: Og the king of Bashan.

Deuteronomy 3:1
Then we turned, and went up the way [north] to Bashan: and Og the king of Bashan came out against us, he and all his people, to battle at Edrei.

Deuteronomy 3:11
For only Og king of Bashan remained of the remnant of giants; behold, his bedstead *was* a bedstead of iron; *is* it not in Rabbath of the children

of Ammon? nine cubits *was* the length thereof, and four cubits the breadth of it, after the cubit of a man.

Og, the king of Bashan, was a remnant of the giants. The Hebrew word used here for giants is the word *rapha*, meaning "giant."[22] The word *rapha* is the singular whereas *rephaim* is the plural. Here, it should be understood in the plural, as its occurrence is referring to the tribe of giants known as the Rephaim.[23] Og, the king of Bashan was the last remaining remnant of the tribe of giants known as the Rephaim.

Og was the king of Bashan and he controlled all the region of Argob, but he actually dwelled within his kingdom in the town of Ashtaroth.

> Deuteronomy 1:4b
> ...and Og the king of Bashan, which dwelt at Ashtaroth in Edrei:

Thus far we have considered giants living at Hebron, which were encountered by the spies sent out by Moses when the children of Israel were camped at Kadesh-barnea. This was when the children of Israel were positioned to enter into the land promised by God to their fathers. This was also before they spent 40 years in the wilderness because of their unbelief and continued rebellion against God.

---

[22] *Strong's Exhaustive Concordance of the Bible*, word # H7497.
[23] See Genesis 14:5

We have also seen another giant that Moses and the children of Israel encountered just before the 40 years in the wilderness were completed and before the nation crossed over the Jordan River to enter into the Promised Land: Og the king of Bashan.

What happened to these giants will be considered in a later chapter. However, there are more records of other tribes of giants in the Bible which we must consider.

Chapter 3.2
Moses Taught About Other Tribes of Giants

So far, the giants we have considered have been living in the city of Hebron and in the town of Ashtaroth, and they were encountered by Moses and the children of Israel before they entered into and occupied the Promised Land. However, while even just these two locations of giants would be noteworthy, there are records of other tribes of giants in the Bible in addition to the Sons of Anak (the Anakims) and the Rephaim.

In the second chapter of Deuteronomy there is a record which bears considering in which Moses told the Israelites the history of the land they were passing through as they journeyed to the Promised Land.

> Deuteronomy 2:4-8
> And command thou the people, saying, Ye *are* to pass through the coast of your brethren the children of Esau, which dwell in Seir; and they shall be afraid of you: take ye good heed unto yourselves therefore:
>
> Meddle not with them; for I will not give you of their land, no, not so much as a foot breadth; because I have given mount Seir unto Esau *for* a possession.
>
> Ye shall buy meat of them for money, that ye may eat; and ye shall also buy water of them for money, that ye may drink.

And when we passed by from our brethren the children of Esau, which dwelt in Seir, through the way of the plain from Elath, and from Eziongaber, we turned and passed by the way of the wilderness of Moab.

As the children of Israel traveled north from Eziongaber (which is roughly 100 miles due south of the Salt Sea and near the coastal waters of the area we today would call the Gulf of Arabia) they came to the land that belonged to the children of Esau known of as Mount Seir, or simply Seir.

As the children of Israel passed by their brethren, they were instructed to be aware that the children of Esau would be afraid of them. Therefore, they were to take good heed unto themselves and not "meddle," or contend, with them. God also told them He would not give them any of their land "no, not so much as a foot breath," because He had given it unto Esau for a possession.

Further instructions from God to the children of Israel included that they were to purchase with money food to eat and water to drink from the children of Esau.

After passing through the coast of Seir, the children of Israel continued north to the land of Moab.

A brief background may help in understanding some of the inhabitants of this area. After fleeing Sodom and Gomorrah, Lot had two sons by his two daughters. The older daughter had a son and named him Moab, meaning "from father," and the younger gave birth to a son and named him Ben-Ammi, meaning "son of my people." The Moabites descended from Moab and the Ammonites descended from Ben-Ammi. They inherited the land given to Lot by God for a possession.

> Deuteronomy 2:9-11
> And the LORD said unto me, Distress not the Moabites, neither contend with them in battle: for I will not give thee of their land *for* a possession; because I have given Ar unto the children of Lot *for* a possession.
>
> The Emims dwelt therein in times past, a people great, and many, and tall, as the Anakims;
>
> Which also were accounted giants, as the Anakims; but the Moabites call them Emims.

After passing by their brethren the children of Esau, the children of Israel continued north up the eastern side of the Salt Sea and passed by the Moabites. God's instructions as they did so were to "distress not the Moabites, neither contend with them in battle" because He had already given Ar unto the children of Lot for a possession. Then Moses went on to expound that a tribe of giants had dwelled there in times past. This tribe of giants was said by Moses to have been, "a people great and many." They were also reported to have been as tall as the Anakims and were considered giants as were the Anakims. They were called the Emims by the Moabites, which means "terrors."[24]

As Moses continues with the record, there is additional insight added.

> Deuteronomy 2:12
> The Horims also dwelt in Seir beforetime; but the children of Esau succeeded them, when they had destroyed them from before them, and dwelt in their stead; as Israel did unto the land of his possession, which the LORD gave unto them.

The Horims are said by some scholars to have been a tribe of giants also, as they are listed here in the context with the Emims and earlier in another record from Genesis which we will consider.[25] However, other than being included in the context here and in Genesis with known tribes of giants, there is no other biblical evidence to conclusively establish that the Horims were giants also.

Let's continue to consider what Moses taught.

> Deuteronomy 2:13-15
> Now rise up, *said I,* and get you over the brook Zered. And we went over the brook Zered.
>
> And the space in which we came from Kadeshbarnea, until we were come over the brook

---

[24] *Strong's Exhaustive Concordance of the Bible,* word # H368.
[25] See Genesis 14:6

Zered, *was* thirty and eight years; until all the generation of the men of war were wasted out from among the host, as the LORD sware unto them.

For indeed the hand of the LORD was against them, to destroy them from among the host, until they were consumed.

The chronological timing of this record is 38 years after the events of Kadesh-barnea when Moses sent the spies into the promised land to spy it out and the events that transpired upon their return.

Deuteronomy 2:16-19
So it came to pass, when all the men of war were consumed and dead from among the people,

That the LORD spake unto me, saying,[26]

Thou art to pass over through Ar, the coast of Moab, this day:

And *when* thou comest nigh over against the children of Ammon, distress them not, nor meddle with them: for I will not give thee of the land of the

---

[26] One can see from Deuteronomy 2:17 that the origin of the information Moses was sharing with the children of Israel was from God, as one can also understand from II Peter 1:20 and 21: "Knowing this first, that no prophecy of the scripture is of any private interpretation. For the prophecy came not in old time by the will of man: but holy men of God spake *as they were* moved by the Holy Ghost." This is how Moses was receiving this historical information.

children of Ammon *any* possession; because I have given it unto the children of Lot *for* a possession.

The town of Ar was located near the northern border of Moab, or "the coast of Moab." As the children of Israel moved north through the land of the Moabites, they could enter either the land of the Amorites or the land of the Ammonites (see Appendix 1). As mentioned previously, the children of Israel were instructed by God to pass through the land of the Moabites and not to distress them because God had already given that land to the children of Lot for an inheritance. In verse 19 of Deuteronomy chapter 2, one can see the same instructions also applied to Israel as they passed through the land of the Ammonites.[27]

---

[27] What has not yet been explained in Deuteronomy chapter 2 is that the Amorites had previously taken part of the land of the Ammonites from the river Arnon north to the river Jabbok. Joshua 12:2 gives the borders of the lands of the Amorites ruled by King Sihon. Please see Appendix 1 for a map which shows these borders.

> Joshua 12:2
> Sihon king of the Amorites, who dwelt in Heshbon, *and* ruled from Aroer, which *is* upon the bank of the river Arnon, and from the middle of the river, and from half Gilead, even unto the river Jabbok, *which is* the border of the children of Ammon;

In verse 2 the southern border of the Amorites is listed as the river Arnon, which was approximately 10 miles north of the city of Ar. Therefore as one journeyed north past Ar in Moab, one would begin to be nearing the northern border, or "coast," of the Moabites. The northern border of the Moabites was separated from the southern border of the Amorites, and the southern border of the Ammonites, by the river Arnon. The northern border of the Amorites was the river Jabbok which was also bordered by the Ammonites.

Deuteronomy 2:19-22

And *when* thou comest nigh over against the children of Ammon, distress them not, nor meddle with them: for I will not give thee of the land of the children of Ammon *any* possession; because I have given it unto the children of Lot *for* a possession.

(That also was accounted a land of giants: giants dwelt therein in old time; and the Ammonites call them Zamzummims;

Moses sought permission from King Sihon to journey through the land of the Amorites but was denied.

Num 21:21-24
And Israel sent messengers unto Sihon king of the Amorites, saying,
Let me pass through thy land: we will not turn into the fields, or into the vineyards; we will not drink *of* the waters of the well: *but* we will go along by the king's *high* way, until we be past thy borders.
And Sihon would not suffer Israel to pass through his border: but Sihon gathered all his people together, and went out against Israel into the wilderness: and he came to Jahaz, and fought against Israel.
And Israel smote him with the edge of the sword, and possessed his land from Arnon unto Jabbok, even unto the children of Ammon: for the border of the children of Ammon *was* strong.

The river Arnon geographically separated the Moabites, on their northern border, from the Amorites and the Ammonites. The river Jabbok was the northern border of the Amorites, separating the Amorites from the Ammonites.

> A people great, and many, and tall, as the Anakims; but the LORD destroyed them before them; and they succeeded them, and dwelt in their stead:

> As he did to the children of Esau, which dwelt in Seir, when he destroyed the Horims from before them; and they succeeded them, and dwelt in their stead even unto this day:

After passing thru Ar and coming to the land of the Ammonites, Moses once again spoke of another tribe of giants, which had lived before "in old time" in their land, and these giants were called by the Ammonites "Zamzummims." He went on to explain the Zamzummims were also giants and "a people great, and many, and tall as the Anakims." Also in verse 22, the Horims are once again spoken of as having been destroyed by God as the Zamzummims were.

Summary

As we have seen, in the days of Moses, there were a number of giants encountered by the children of Israel and taught about by Moses. Initially, as the spies sent out by Moses explored the Promised Land, they encountered some of the sons of Anak who were identified as Ahiman, Sheshai, and Talmai.

Thirty-eight years later, as Moses led the children of Israel north from the southeastern area of the Salt Sea, he related to the children of Israel the history of the inhabitants of the land they were passing through. He told them of two tribes of giants which had previously lived there. He spoke of the Emims, who previously lived in the land then occupied by the Moabites, and the Zamzummims, who previously lived in the land then occupied by the Ammonites. He also made mention of the Horims who had been succeeded by the descendants of Esau.

Moses went on to explain that both the Emims and the Zamzummims were indeed tribes of giants as he described them both to have been "a people great, and many and tall as the Anakims." Of the Emims, he added they "were accounted giants, as the Anakims." Some scholars have put forth that the Horims may have been giants as well.

Interestingly, the Anakims appear to have been the standard that the other tribes of giants were measured against, since Moses compared both the Emims and Zamzummims to them. This may be due to the fact that the Anakims were the giants that the nation of Israel initially encountered during their exploration from Kadesh-barnea.

Although Moses and the children of Israel did not encounter any of the Emims, Zamzummims, or Horims since they had already been destroyed before the time of Moses, as they later journeyed north they did encounter another giant, whom we previously considered, Og the king of Bashan, the last living remnant of another tribe of giants known as the Rephaim.

Chapter 3.3
Giants in the Days of Abraham

There is a record in Genesis chapter 14 from the time of Abraham,[28] which would have occurred more than 400 years prior to the record previously considered in Deuteronomy which spoke of Moses' time. This record from Genesis provides more information about the giants referred to by Moses in Deuteronomy chapter 2.

In this record from Genesis chapter 14, a war occurred. There were four kings from the Mesopotamian area that went to war with five kings inhabiting the area south and east of the Salt Sea (also known as the cities of the plain).

Genesis 14:1-12
And it came to pass in the days of Amraphel king of Shinar, Arioch king of Ellasar, Chedorlaomer king of Elam, and Tidal king of nations;

That these made war with Bera king of Sodom, and with Birsha king of Gomorrah, Shinab king of Admah, and Shemeber king of Zeboiim, and the king of Bela, which is Zoar.

All these were joined together in the vale of Siddim, which is the salt sea.

---

[28] In Genesis 17:5 God changes Abram's name to Abraham. For the sake of simplicity and familiarity, the more commonly used name of Abraham will be used throughout this study, except for the quoted scripture passages.

Twelve years they served Chedorlaomer, and in the thirteenth year they rebelled.

And in the fourteenth year came Chedorlaomer, and the kings that were with him, and smote the Rephaims in Ashteroth Karnaim, and the Zuzims in Ham, and the Emims in Shaveh Kiriathaim,

And the Horites in their mount Seir, unto Elparan, which is by the wilderness.

And they returned, and came to Enmishpat, which is Kadesh, and smote all the country of the Amalekites, and also the Amorites, that dwelt in Hazezontamar.

And there went out the king of Sodom, and the king of Gomorrah, and the king of Admah, and the king of Zeboiim, and the king of Bela (the same is Zoar;) and they joined battle with them in the vale of Siddim;

With Chedorlaomer the king of Elam, and with Tidal king of nations, and Amraphel king of Shinar, and Arioch king of Ellasar; four kings with five.

And the vale of Siddim was full of slimepits; and the kings of Sodom and Gomorrah fled, and fell there; and they that remained fled to the mountain.

And they took all the goods of Sodom and Gomorrah, and all their victuals, and went their way.

And they took Lot, Abram's brother's son, who dwelt in Sodom, and his goods, and departed.

The five kings of the cities of the plain had served Chedorlaomer, King of Elam (a region just east of Babylon), for 12 years. In the 13th year they rebelled from their servitude, and in the 14th year Chedorlaomer came from Mesopotamia with three other kings and their armies to punish them for their rebellion.

The four kings and their armies went to fight the five kings of the cities of the plain. The four kings first traveled north-northwest from the Mesopotamian area along the trade route that parallels the Euphrates River before turning south into the area that would later be known as Syria. They took this route to the land of Canaan most likely to avoid traveling through the extremely harsh deserts and mountainous terrain that separated the lush areas of the cities of the plains south and east of the Salt Sea from the fertile Mesopotamian area.

As the four kings and their armies approached the area of the Salt Sea (which is referred to today as the Dead Sea), they came from the north and worked their way southward, making war on the inhabitants they encountered until they finally came to the Vale of Siddim at the southern end of the Salt Sea. There the four kings from the Mesopotamian area defeated the five kings from the cities of the plain.[29]

---

[29] The exact locations inhabited and ruled by the five kings living in the cities of the plain have yet to be discovered and remain unknown. It is generally believed they lived in the region south and east of the Salt Sea. The Vale, or valley, of Siddim, where the four kings from the

47

The record from Genesis chapter 14 primarily deals with the defeat of the five kings of the cities of the plain and the carrying away of the people and their possessions from the cities of this area, which included Lot and his family. Lot was Abraham's brother's son who had traveled with him from Haran.

Genesis 14:13-16
And there came one that had escaped, and told Abram the Hebrew; for he dwelt in the plain of Mamre the Amorite, brother of Eshcol, and brother of Aner: and these were confederate with Abram.

And when Abram heard that his brother was taken captive, he armed his trained servants, born in his own house, three hundred and eighteen, and pursued them unto Dan.

And he divided himself against them, he and his servants, by night, and smote them, and pursued them unto Hobah, which is on the left hand of Damascus.

And he brought back all the goods, and also brought again his brother Lot, and his goods, and the women also, and the people.

Mesopotamian area defeated the five kings inhabiting the cities of the plain, also remains undiscovered. Siddim is thought to have been located in the valley at the southern end of the Salt Sea where modern bitumen deposits have been found in respect to the slime pits mentioned in Genesis 14:10. Some scholars believe the actual location to be currently submerged under the southern area of the Salt Sea, or the Dead Sea.

Abraham and 318 of his servants born and trained in his own house pursued the four kings as they were on their way northward back to their own kingdoms, overtaking them in the area north of the Sea of Chinnereth (the Sea of Galilee) known as Dan. There they attacked the armies of the four kings by night and defeated them, killing Chedorlaomer and routing the armies of the four kings as far northward as Damascus. This was a remarkable victory considering the amount of damage inflicted by the armies of the four kings as they moved throughout the area, and it was accomplished by just Abraham and his 318 trained servants.[30]

---

[30] Genesis 14:13 states that Abraham was in alliance three Amorites: "for he [Abraham] dwelt in the plain of Mamre the Amorite, brother of Eshcol, and brother of Aner: and these *were* confederate with Abram." One can clearly see in verse 15 that it was Abraham and his servants who defeated the four kings.

> Genesis 14:15
> And he divided himself against them, he and his servants, by night, and smote them, and pursued them unto Hobah, which *is* on the left hand of Damascus.

However, at the conclusion of the account in Genesis 14, in verses 22 through 24, it appears that men from their alliance accompanied Abraham and his 318 trained servants.

> Genesis 14:24
> Save only that which the young men have eaten, and the portion of the men which went with me, Aner, Eshcol, and Mamre; let them take their portion.

Although Abraham and his 318 trained servants were the ones who defeated the four Kings, it does appear they were accompanied by men from his alliance with Aner, Eshcol and Mamre.

WHAT ABOUT GIANTS IN THE BIBLE?

Although the Scriptures do not explicitly state what type of training Abraham's servants had received, one could logically reason it was beyond shepherding and domestic household duties in order to have so thoroughly defeated the four armies in one night. Afterward, they returned home with Lot and his family and all of the goods and people that they recovered.

We've considered this entire record to provide the context for verses 5 and 6.

> Genesis 14:5-6
> And in the fourteenth year came Chedorlaomer, and the kings that *were* with him, and smote the **Rephaims in Ashtaroth Karnaim**, and the **Zuzims in Ham**, and the **Emims in Shaveh Kiriathaim** [emphasis added],
>
> And the **Horites in their mount Seir** [emphasis added], unto Elparan, which *is* by the wilderness.

It was previously established in Deuteronomy chapters 2 and 3 that some, if not all, of the tribes mentioned here in Genesis 14:5 and 6 were tribes of giants.

Let's consider each of these tribes listed that the four kings destroyed, utilizing the records from Deuteronomy to gain more information about each tribe.

The Rephaims

Genesis 14:5-6
And in the fourteenth year came Chedorlaomer, and the kings that *were* with him, and smote the **Rephaims in Ashtaroth Karnaim** [emphasis added], and the Zuzims in Ham, and the Emims in Shaveh Kiriathaim,

And the Horites in their mount Seir, unto Elparan, which *is* by the wilderness.

As previously seen, *rephaim* is the plural of the Hebrew word *rapha*, meaning giants. The Rephaim in Ashtaroth Karnaim were a tribe of giants. We have already seen from Deuteronomy chapter 3 when reading about Og, the king of Bashan, that he also lived in the town of Ashtaroth, and he was the only one that remained as a remnant of the Rephaim giants at the time of Moses.

The Zuzims

Also mentioned in Genesis 14:5 are the Zuzims in Ham.

Gen 14:5-6
And in the fourteenth year came Chedorlaomer, and the kings that *were* with him, and smote the Rephaims in Ashtaroth Karnaim, and the **Zuzims in Ham** [emphasis added], and the Emims in Shaveh Kiriathaim,

51

And the Horites in their mount Seir, unto Elparan, which *is* by the wilderness.

The Zuzims are believed by many scholars to be the same tribe of giants as the Zamzummims mentioned by Moses in Deuteronomy 2:20. This would be of particular interest as neither the Zuzims nor the Zamzummims are mentioned elsewhere again in the Bible.

Easton's Bible Dictionary of 1897 identifies the Zuzims as being the Zamzummims, according to some scholars. Also, *The Jewish Encyclopedia of 1906* says regarding this passage and of the Zuzims:

> The narrator must have supposed that the Zuzim were well known, for he prefixes the definite article to their name, though its use may also imply that even to him the nation was somewhat nebulous. This prefix induced the Septuagint and the Peshiṭta (or the scribe of the copy underlying their version) to read the name as an appellative. They therefore translate it as 'the strong' (= 'ha'izzuzim') or 'the mighty' (= 'ha-'ezuzim'), and thus identify the people with the Rephaim, the giants who occupied the district and who are said to have been called 'Zamzummim' by the Ammonites (Deut. ii. 20). The rendering of Symmachus results from a combination of the two names Zuzim and Zamzummim (Σοαζομμειν), and thus anticipates those modern scholars who maintain that the names are identical, the variance being due to scribal errors.

The town of Ham, where the Zuzims were destroyed, was geographically located at the northern edge of the land of the Ammonites, which would place the Zuzims living in approximately the same area as the Zamzummims described by Moses in Deuteronomy 2:20. This would have been in an area with the Rephaim to the north and the Emims to the south. (See Appendix 1)

> Deuteronomy 2:18-22
> Thou art to pass over through Ar, the coast of Moab, this day:
>
> And *when* thou comest nigh over against the children of Ammon, distress them not, nor meddle with them: for I will not give thee of the land of the children of Ammon *any* possession; because I have given it unto the children of Lot *for* a possession.
>
> (That also was accounted a land of giants: giants dwelt therein in old time; and the Ammonites call them Zamzummims;
>
> A people great, and many, and tall, as the Anakims; but the LORD destroyed them before them; and they succeeded them, and dwelt in their stead:
>
> As he did to the children of Esau, which dwelt in Seir, when he destroyed the Horims from before them; and they succeeded them, and dwelt in their stead even unto this day:

The Emims

Genesis 14:5-6
And in the fourteenth year came Chedorlaomer, and
the kings that *were* with him, and smote the
Rephaims in Ashtaroth Karnaim, and the Zuzims in
Ham, and the **Emims in Shaveh Kiriathaim**
[emphasis added],

And the Horites in their mount Seir, unto Elparan,
which *is* by the wilderness.

Another group the four kings destroyed, the Emims in
Shaveh Kiriathaim, referred to in Genesis 14:5, are the
same Emims Moses spoke of in Deuteronomy chapter 2
verses 10 and 11. Moses, by revelation, referred to them as
"a people great, and many, and tall, as the Anakims; which
also were accounted as giants, as the Anakims; but the
Moabites call them Emims."

Shaveh Kiriathaim, where the Emims were said to be, is
identified in *The Treasury of Scriptural Knowledge* to have
been the "plains of Kiriathaim." The plains of Kiriathaim
are identified as being east of the Jordan River, 10 miles
westward from Medeba, and afterwards belonging to
Sihon, king of Heshbon. Although in the days of Moses this
is a few miles north of the border of Moab, it is only
slightly north of there and certainly within the vicinity
spoken of by Moses in Deuteronomy.

The Horites

In Genesis 14:6, it also says the four kings smote the "Horites in their mount Seir."

> Gen 14:5-6
> And in the fourteenth year came Chedorlaomer, and the kings that *were* with him, and smote the Rephaims in Ashtaroth Karnaim, and the Zuzims in Ham, and the Emims in Shaveh Kiriathaim,
>
> And the **Horites in their mount Seir** [emphasis added], unto Elparan, which *is* by the wilderness.

The Emims that we just examined were spoken of by Moses in Deuteronomy 2:10-11, and in verse 12, the Horims are mentioned, which we will see is the same tribe described in Genesis 14:6 as the Horites.

> Deuteronomy 2:12
> The Horims also dwelt in Seir beforetime; but the children of Esau succeeded them, when they had destroyed them from before them, and dwelt in their stead; as Israel did unto the land of his possession, which the LORD gave unto them.

In Deuteronomy 2:12 the Horims are referred to as, "The Horims [who] also dwelt in Seir." This is the same tribe referred to in Genesis 14:6 as, "the Horites in their mount Seir." Although the names are slightly different ("Horim" and "Horite"), these can be understood to be the same tribe because they are both described as inhabiting the same place: Seir or Mount Seir.

One cannot definitively say if the Horites were a tribe of giants, but they are listed here as another tribe that the four kings destroyed.

In verses 19 through 22 of Deuteronomy chapter 2, the Zamzummims were said to have been destroyed by the Lord and succeeded by the Ammonites as He (the Lord) also did to the children of Esau, which dwelt in Seir, when He destroyed the Horims. From this record in Deuteronomy chapter 2, one can see the Zamzummims were destroyed as the Horims were destroyed. In Genesis chapter 14, the Zuzims and the Horites both were destroyed by the four kings and their armies when they came from the Mesopotamian area. This would appear to biblically connect the Zuzims as being the Zamzummims and the Horites as being the Horims by way of the record in Genesis 14.

Summary

From the record in Genesis 14 during the days and time of Abraham, there were at least three tribes of giants referred to: the Rephaim, the Emims, and the Zuzims. As the four kings from the Mesopotamian area moved south to eventually battle the five kings from the cities of the plain, they destroyed these three tribes of giants in succession: the Rephaims in Astheroth, the Zuzims in Ham, and the Emims in Shaveh Kiriathaim.

Two of these tribes of giants lived in the lands that were later given to Lot as an inheritance: the Emims, who occupied the land later known of as Moab, and the Zamzummims, who occupied the land later known of as the land of the Ammonites.

The Zamzummims and the Horims referred to by Moses in Deuteronomy chapter 2 are also referred to as the Zuzims and the Horites in Genesis chapter 14.

Another point worth mentioning here is how well established the different tribes of giants were by the time of Abraham. There were the Anakims living in the city of Kirjatharba (which we have seen was established before the time of Abraham), the Rephaim living in Ashteroth Karnaim, the Zamzummims/Zuzims living in the land later inhabited by the Ammonites, and the Emims living in the land later inhabited by the Moabites. Abraham was born less than 300 years after the Flood, and by this point in time, giants were established into at least four different tribes inhabiting four different geographic areas. It also appears that after the Flood, each tribe of giants was the original possessor of the land they inhabited, as there are no biblical records of anyone living in the lands they inhabited before them.

How rich this makes the record of Abraham and his 318 servants, as we realize that the four kings they pursued and overtook had just destroyed many tribes, including at least three well-established tribes of not just ordinary strong men, but giants. The four kings were indeed a formidable force, and yet the man of God, Abraham, and his comparably small group of servants were victorious in the face of such incredible opposition.

Chapter 3.4
Giants in the Days of David

We have considered giants in the days of Moses and Abraham, but there are also giants spoken of in the Bible who lived later during the life of David.

Although we will consider later in more detail what happened to the giants, there is a verse in the book of Joshua that bears our consideration now.

> Joshua 11:22
> There was none of the Anakims left in the land of the children of Israel: only in Gaza, in Gath, and in Ashdod, there remained.

After the nation of Israel, led by Joshua, entered into and took possession of the Promised Land, all of the tribe of giants known as the Anakims were either killed or chased out of the land. However, as verse 22 of Joshua chapter 11 reveals, there were still Anakims living in the neighboring areas of Gaza, Gath, and Ashdod. Many years after the days of Joshua, during the days of David, all of these towns were under the political and governmental control of the Philistines.

Of all the giants recorded in God's Word, the one most widely known of today is probably Goliath, who was from the town of Gath. This is primarily due to there being such a detailed description of his actions against the army of the

Lord, his size and armament, and David's heroic actions as well.

> I Samuel 17:1-4
>
> Now the Philistines gathered together their armies to battle, and were gathered together at Shochoh, which *belongeth* to Judah, and pitched between Shochoh and Azekah, in Ephesdammim.
>
> And Saul and the men of Israel were gathered together, and pitched by the valley of Elah, and set the battle in array against the Philistines.
>
> And the Philistines stood on a mountain on the one side, and Israel stood on a mountain on the other side: and *there was* a valley between them.
>
> And there went out a champion out of the camp of the Philistines, named Goliath, of Gath, whose height *was* six cubits and a span.

Although Goliath is probably the most famous of all the giants recorded in the Bible, it is most interesting that the Scriptures do not specifically identify him as a giant or an Anakim. However, the detailed description of his size alone would confirm this to be the case. He was also from the town of Gath, which Joshua chapter 11 stated many years prior was one of the towns where Anakims were known to be living.

Goliath was not the only giant encountered by David and company. David's encounter with Goliath occurred when he was only a teenager. He once again came up against another giant in battle when he was 60 years of age.[31]

> II Samuel 21:15-17
> Moreover the Philistines had yet war again with Israel; and David went down, and his servants with him, and fought against the Philistines: and David waxed faint.
>
> And Ishbibenob, which *was* of the sons of the giant, the weight of whose spear *weighed* three hundred *shekels* of brass in weight, he being girded with a new *sword,* thought to have slain David.
>
> But Abishai the son of Zeruiah succoured him, and smote the Philistine, and killed him. Then the men of David sware unto him, saying, Thou shalt go no more out with us to battle, that thou quench not the light of Israel.

As David grew fatigued in battle, the giant Ishbibenob thought to take advantage of him and kill him. Yet, one of David's mighty men, Abishai, intervened and killed the giant. From this point forward, David's men would no longer allow him to go out with them into battle.

---

[31] *The Companion Bible*, Dr. Bullinger notes on page 389 in reference to I Samuel 17:12, that David was between 16 and 17 years of age when he killed Goliath. Also from *The Companion Bible*, page 438, note on the verse from II Samuel 21:15, Dr. Bullinger identifies the time of the battles recorded in II Samuel 21:15, and following verses, was 930-923 BC and that David was 60 years of age when he went up against Isbibenob.

II Samuel 21:18-21

And it came to pass after this, that there was again a battle with the Philistines at Gob: then Sibbechai the Hushathite slew Saph, which *was* of the sons of the giant.

And there was again a battle in Gob with the Philistines, where Elhanan the son of Jaareoregim, a Bethlehemite, slew *the brother of* Goliath the Gittite, the staff of whose spear *was* like a weaver's beam.

And there was yet a battle in Gath, where was a man of *great* stature, that had on every hand six fingers, and on every foot six toes, four and twenty in number; and he also was born to the giant.

And when he defied Israel, Jonathan the son of Shimea the brother of David slew him.

These four were born to the giant in Gath, and fell by the hand of David, and by the hand of his servants.

In all there were four giants "born to the giant in Gath" who is unnamed. This certainly lends credence to the understanding of family genetics involved. The four giants "born to the giant in Gath" were Ishbibenob, Saph, one identified as "the brother of" Goliath, and another unnamed giant identified by having six fingers on each hand and six toes on each foot. Interestingly, six fingers on each hand and six toes on each foot is also a genetic mutation.

Including Goliath, who David killed while a teenager, and the four other giants killed later by David and company, there were at least five giants encountered during the life of David. All were from the town of Gath, and all appear to be of the same genetic family.

Part 4
How Large Were the Giants?

In discussing the topic of giants, the conversation invariably comes around to a question such as, "How large were they?" The answer to this question, in part, begins with understanding that just like people today, the giants all varied in height, weight, girth, and so on. No two were exactly the same.

Chapter 4.1
Biblical Weights and Measurements;
How Long is a Cubit, and How Heavy is a Shekel?

In order to understand how large the giants were, one first needs to consider the system of measurements used in the Bible. Originally, measurements of length were derived from the human body: the arm, hand, finger and foot.[32] The span of the hand across from extended thumb to little finger extended and the length of the stride while walking were other measurements of linear distance.

The cubit is a primary unit of measurement in the Bible. It is a unit of linear measurement based on the length of the arm from the elbow to the tip of the middle finger. It is first mentioned in the Bible in the book of Genesis when God gave the instructions to Noah concerning the dimensions of the Ark. Regrettably, the cubit rod used by Noah and sons when building the Ark has not survived for posterity's sake.

One of the problems of using parts of the body for measurement is that the parts differ in length from one individual to another. Therefore, the measurements, by necessity, needed to be standardized. This standardization differed from one country to another and from one culture to another. For example, in ancient Egypt a number of cubit rods were discovered in tombs. Each cubit rod is divided into palms, each palm being further divided into fingers, and the fingers being further subdivided still. These cubit

---

[32] http://jewishencyclopedia.com/articles/14821-weights-and-measures

rods vary in length from 20.6 inches to 20.8 inches.[33] Historically, the cubit ranged from 17 to 22 inches depending on the culture. As archaic as this system of measuring may appear to us today with digital and laser measuring systems, this was one of the tools that enabled the Egyptians to construct the near-perfect pyramids of Giza.

Although the cubit varied in length from one culture to another, the majority of sources indicate that the 18-inch cubit is the best modern interpretation of the historical Biblical length.[34] The Torah lists the length of the cubit as being about 18 inches.[35] Many other explanations of measurement list the cubit as being 18 inches also, as measured from the elbow to the end of the middle finger, one "span" as being 9 inches from the end of the thumb extended to the end of the little finger extended (also considered one half of a cubit), and one "hand" as being 4 inches, which is still used to measure the height of horses today.[36]

---

[33] Marshall Clagett (1999) *Ancient Egyptian Science, A Source Book. Volume Three: Ancient Egyptian Mathematics.* Philadelphia: American Philosophical Society ISBN 978-0-87169-232-0.

[34] "Cubit", Encyclopedia Britannica, 10-15-2016, http://www.britannica.com/EBchecked/topic/145781/cubit.

[35] W. Gunter Plaut, Bernard J. Banaberger, William W. Hallo, *The Torah*, New York: Union Of American Hebrew Congregations 1981. Footnote to Genesis 6:15.

[36] *New Franklin Arithmetic: Second Book* by Edwin Pliny (1895) Butler, Sheldon & Co., page 384; and *The Principles of Arithmetic* by Daniel O'Sullivan (1872) page. 69

The most detailed record of the height of a giant comes from the account of when David slew Goliath, recorded in I Samuel 17.

> I Samuel 17:4
> And there went out a champion out of the camp of the Philistines, named Goliath, of Gath, whose height *was* six cubits and a span.

A cubit being 18 inches and a span being one half of a cubit, or 9 inches, means Goliath would have been about 9 feet 9 inches tall, only 3 inches shy of 10 feet. But what is most interesting is that in this record even greater detail is placed upon the weight of his weapons and armor, which would be indicative of his strength in addition to his height.

> I Samuel 17:5-7
> And *he had* an helmet of brass upon his head, and he *was* armed with a coat of mail; and the weight of the coat *was* five thousand shekels of brass.
>
> And *he had* greaves of brass upon his legs, and a target of brass between his shoulders.
>
> And the staff of his spear *was* like a weaver's beam; and his spear's head *weighed* six hundred shekels of iron: and one bearing a shield went before him.

The shekel is a unit of weight that was used for trading before the advent of coins. It was the common unit of measurement and was used predominately throughout the region of Palestine from the Mediterranean Sea to as far eastward as Mesopotamia. As with the cubit, the shekel had some variance depending on era, government, and region. During the days of David, the weight of the shekel is believed to be no less than 11 grams, or approximately 0.388 ounces. Using this as the weight of the shekel, the weight of Goliath's coat of mail would have been about 121 pounds, and the weight of the spear's head approximately 12 pounds.[37,38]

In addition to the coat of mail, Goliath also wore a helmet of brass upon his head and greaves of brass upon his legs. The greaves of brass would be similar to brass shin guards worn over the front of the legs from just below the knee to just above the ankle. They were worn to prevent any blows on the lower leg from breaking the bone that is protected only by skin. He also wore a "target of brass" between his shoulders. This would be brass protection worn on his chest to prevent any arrows, spears, or swords from piercing his chest and to protect the vital organs that are there.

Goliath must have been a fierce and intimidating sight to behold standing almost 10 feet tall and armored with brass as he was. With someone bearing a shield before him, he would have seemed to most in that day and time as the ultimate weapon and an insurmountable force—to most, but not to all.

---

[37] Dilke, Oswald Ashton Wentworth (1987) *Mathematics and Measurement,* University of California Press, p.46
[38] Wiseman, Donald J. (1958) *Illustrations from Biblical Archaeology,* London: Tyndale Press pp 87-89

Although there are no other giants in the Bible whose height and armor are covered in such detail as Goliath, there is another giant whose size was described by the size of his bed.

> Deuteronomy 3:11
> For only Og king of Bashan remained of the remnant of giants [Rephaim]; behold, his bedstead *was* a bedstead of iron; *is* it not in Rabbath of the children of Ammon? nine cubits *was* the length thereof, and four cubits the breadth of it, after the cubit of a man.

Once again, using 18 inches for a cubit would have made the bed of Og the giant 13 feet 6 inches long and 6 feet wide. By comparison, a modern day king-size bed is just 6 feet 8 inches long and 6 feet 4 inches wide.

Although Goliath of Gath is probably the most famous of all the giants recorded in the Bible, it appears he may not have been the largest. (See Appendix 2)

Chapter 4.2
Is There Any Archeological Evidence of Giants?

When considering the size of the giants, it sheds considerable light to look at modern day archaeological findings, which include giant skeletons unearthed beginning from the middle of the 19th century. Sadly, one cannot go to a wing of the Smithsonian museum to view archeological remains of giants today. However, this does not mean that there have not been archeological discoveries of giants.

One of the best documented and most widely known archeological findings of giant remains happened in the early 1890s. Press accounts mention a discovery of human bones at a prehistoric site at Montpellier, France. The bones were dated from the Neolithic Period and were undeniably human. The journal and photo engravings (this was before the advent of modern day photography) were of numerous skulls, humeri, and tibiae that belonged to a race of men between 10 and 15 feet in height. The bones were reportedly sent to the Paris Academy for further study.[39,40,41]

The Neolithic time period is significant for its "megalithic" architecture such as Stonehenge and the Egyptian Pyramids of Giza. This time period would generally coincide biblically to the time from the creation of Adam up through

---

[39] "Le gent de Castelnau" La Nature 20(992): 142. June 4, 1892
[40] "A Race of Giants in Old Gaul" The Popular Science News and Boston Journal of Chemistry and Pharmacy 24 (8):113. August 1890
[41] The Princeton Union" (Princeton Minn.) pg. 2. October 11, 1894

the time of Abraham, as archaeologists and anthropologists date the Neolithic time period from 9,000 BC to 2,000 BC.[42,43,44]

The New York Times Archives contain the press release mentioned above, and in addition, at least 18 other press releases of archeological discoveries of giant human remains that were written about from 1856 to 1916, some of which are listed below. There are also numerous other articles from various publications that reference remains of giants, some of which are also included below.

The first such article included is from November 21, 1856.

THE NEW YORK TIMES, NOVEMBER 21, 1856
SKELETON OF A GIANT FOUND.

A day or two since, some workmen engaged in subsoiling the grounds of Sheriff WICKHAN, at his vineyard in East Wheeling, came across a human skeleton. Although much decayed, there was little difficulty in identifying it, by placing the bones, which could not have belonged to others than a human body, in their original position. The impression made by the skeleton in the earth, and the skeleton itself, were measured by the Sheriff

---

[42] Bahn, P. "The New Penguin Dictionary of Archaeology. Penguin, 2005

[43] Darvill, T. "Concise Oxford Dictionary of Archaeology". Oxford University Press, 2009

[44] Renfrew, C. "Archeology: Theories, Methods, and Practice (Sixth Edition)". Thames & Hudson, 2012

and a brother in the craft locale, both of whom were prepared to swear that it was *ten feet nine inches in length*. Its jaws and teeth were almost as large as those of a horse. The bones are to be seen at the Sheriff's office. – *Wheeling Times*.

THE BOSTON MEDICAL AND SURGICAL JOURNAL, JUNE 19, 1856
MEDICAL INTELLIGENCE

Western Giants in their Slumber.—The Burlington (Iowa) State Gazette says that while some workmen were engaged in excavating for the cellar of Governor Grimes's new building, on the corner of Maine and Valley streets, they came upon an arched vault some ten feet square, which, on being opened, was found to contain eight human skeletons of gigantic proportions. The walls of the vault were about fourteen inches thick, well laid up with cement or indestructible mortar. The vault is about six feet deep from the base to the arch. The skeletons are in a good state of preservation, and we venture to say are the largest human remains ever found, being a little over eight feet long.--*Calendar* (Hartford).

THE NEW YORK TIMES, DECEMBER 25, 1868
REPORTED DISCOVERY OF A HUGE SKELETON.

From the Sank Rapids (Minn.) Sentinel, Dec. 18.

Day before yesterday, while the quarrymen employed by the Sank Rapids Water Power Company were engaged in quarrying rock for the dam which is being erected across the Mississippi, at this place, found imbedded in the solid granite rock the remains of a human being of gigantic status. About seven feet below the surface of the ground, and about three feet and a half beneath the upper stratum of rock, the remains were found imbedded in sand, which evidently had been placed in the quadrangular grave which had been dug out of the rock to receive the last remains of this antediluvian giant. The grave was twelve feet in length, four feet wide, and about three feet in depth, and is to-day at least two feet below the present level of the river. The remains are completely petrified, and are of gigantic dimensions. The head is massive, measuring thirty-one and one-half inches in circumference, but low in the *asfrontis*, and very flat on top. The Femur measures twenty-six and a quarter inches, and the Fibula twenty-five and a half, while the body is equally long in proportion. From the crown of the head to the sole of the foot, the length is ten feet nine and a half inches. The giant must have weighed at least 900 pounds when covered with a reasonable amount of flesh. The petrified remains, and there is nothing left but the naked bones, now weigh 304¼ pounds. The thumb and fingers of the left hand, and the left foot from the ankle to the toes are gone; but all the other parts are perfect. Over the sepulchre of the unknown dead was placed a large, flat limestone rock that remained perfectly separated from the surrounding granite rock.

OHIO DEMOCRAT, JANUARY 14, 1870
CARDIFF GIANT UNDONE WITH AN ENORMOUS IRON HELMET

On Tuesday morning last, while Mr. William Thompson, assisted by Mr. Robert R. Smith, was engaged in making an excavation near the house of the former, about half a mile north of West Hickory, preparatory to erecting a derrick, they exhumed an enormous helmet of iron, which was corroded with rust.

Further digging brought to light a sword, which measured nine feet in length. Curiosity incited them to enlarge the hole, and after some little time they discovered the bones of two enormous feet. Following up the "lead" they had so unexpectedly struck, in a few hours' time they had unearthed the well-preserved remains of an enormous giant, belonging to a species of the human family, which probably inhabited this and other parts of the world, at the time of which the Bible speaks when it says: "And there were giants in those days."

The helmet is said to be of the shape of those among the ruins of Nineveh. The bones of the skeleton are a remarkable white. The teeth are all in their places and all of extraordinary size. These relics have been taken to Tionesta where they are visited by large numbers of people daily.

When his "giantship" was in the flesh he must have stood eighteen feet tall in his stockings. These remarkable relics will be shipped to New York early next week. The joints of the skeleton are now being glued together. These remains were found about twelve feet under the surface of a mound, which had been thrown up probably centuries ago, and which was not more than three feet above the level of the ground around it.

TORONTO, ONTARIO, *DAILY TELEGRAPH*, AUGUST 23, 1871
NIAGARA'S ANCIENT CEMETERY OF GIANTS
A REMARKABLE SIGHT: TWO HUNDRED SKELETONS IN CAYUGA TOWNSHIP

A SINGULAR DISCOVERY BY A TORONTONIAN AND OTHERS—A VAST GOLGOTHA OPENED TO VIEW—SOME REMAINS OF THE "GIANTS THAT WERE IN THOSE DAYS" FROM OUR OWN CORRESPONDENTS.

On Wednesday last, Rev. Nathaniel Wardell, Messers Orin Wardell (of Toronto), and Daniel Fredenburg were digging on the farm of the latter gentleman, which is on the banks of the Grand River, in the township of Cayuga.

When they got to five or six feet below the surface, a strange sight met them. Piled in layers, one upon top of the other, were some two hundred skeletons of human beings nearly perfect: around the neck of each one being a string of beads.

There were also deposited in this pit a number of axes and skimmers made of stone. In the jaws of several of the skeletons were large stone pipes, one of which Mr. O. Wardell took with him to Toronto a day or two after this Golgotha was unearthed.

These skeletons are those of men of gigantic stature, some of them measuring nine feet, very few of them being less than seven feet. Some of the thigh bones were found to be at least a foot longer than those at present known, and one of the skulls being examined completely covered the head of an ordinary person.

These skeletons are supposed to belong to those of a race of people anterior to the Indians.

MIDDLESEX, UK, *CENTRAL PRESS*,
NOVEMBER 26, 1873
MONSTROUS!

Some interesting discoveries have just been made in
a cave called, "King Solomon's Cave", Montana,
United States, and an account of them is given by a
correspondent of the *Deer Lodge Independent* who
formed one of a party of explorers of the cave in
question. After crawling through several narrow
passages into a "most magnificent chamber", the
attention of the explorers was attracted by a massive
shield made of copper 57 inches in length and 36
inches in width leaning against the wall; about 10
feet beyond the shield, and eight feet from the floor,
was a cavity in the wall. One of the party by the aid
of some stones, climbed up to the aperture with a
light but quickly descended in such a state of alarm
that he was for some moments unable to explain
that in the niche lay a petrified giant. The other
explorers immediately climbed up to the aperture
and gazed in. There, sure enough, was the monster
man, whose dimensions on measurement were 9
feet 7 and a half inches, 38 inches across the breast
and two feet deep. A helmet of brass or copper of
gigantic proportions was on his head which, "the
corrosive elements of time had sealed to his brow".
He seems to have been a "disagreeable customer",
and it is perhaps as well that he is dead and
petrified, for near him were two mammoth
spearheads, one of them with a socket of silver, into

which to insert a large pole or handle. There was also a large hook made of bone, apparently manufactured from the tusk of a "leviathan of the land". On the wall were some strange looking letters and pictures of three ships, each having three masts, the middle mast being only two thirds the height of the outward ones. There was also on a flat stone in the wall the picture of a large man with a spear in his hand, and of another ship. On removing this stone, another chamber was discovered, in which were the bones of several more giants, a primitive quartz crusher, and a number of tools made of copper. It is supposed that these poor giants were at work a thousand years ago in the cave when a slide from the mountain above immured them in a living tomb. The search is to be further prosecuted; and in the meantime the explorers are described as "almost wild with the strange and curious things" they have discovered. This beats the "sea serpent" to fits.--*Pall Mall Gazette.*

SCIENTIFIC AMERICAN, AUGUST 14, 1880
ANCIENT AMERICAN GIANTS

The Rev. Stephen Bowers notes in the *Kansas City Review of Science* the opening of an interesting mound in Bush Creek Township, Ohio. The mound was opened by the Historical Society of the township, under the immediate supervision of Dr. J. E. Everhart of Zanesville.

It measured 65 by 34 feet at the summit, gradually sloping in every direction and was 8 feet in height.

There was found in it a sort of clay coffin including the skeleton of a woman measuring 8 feet in length. Within this coffin was found also a child about 3 and a half feet in length and an image that crumbled when exposed to the atmosphere.

In another grave was found the skeleton of a man and a woman, the former measuring nine and the latter 8 feet in length. In a third cave occurred two other skeletons, male and female, measuring respectively nine feet four inches and eight feet.

Seven other skeletons were found in the mound, the smallest of which measured eight feet, while others reached the enormous length of ten feet. They were buried singly or each in separate graves. Resting against one of the coffins was an engraved stone tablet (now in Cincinnati) from the characters on which Dr. Everhart and Mr. Bowers are led to conclude that this giant race were sun worshipers.

PHILADELPHIA TIMES, JUNE 27, 1885
GIANTS FOUND ON THE NEW YORK-PENNSYLVANIA STATE LINE

"Why this man was ten or twelve feet high."

WHAT ABOUT GIANTS IN THE BIBLE?

"Thunder and lightning!" exclaimed Mr. Porter in astonishment. The first speaker, who has won local distinction as a scientist, reiterated his assertion.

J. H. Porter has a farm near Northeast, not many miles from where the Lake Shore Railroad crosses the New York state boundary line. Early this week some workmen in Mr. Porter's employ came upon the entrance to a cave and on entering it found heaps of human bones within. Many skeletons were complete and specimens of the find were brought out and exhibited to the naturalists and archaeologists of the neighborhood. They informed the wondering bystanders that the remains were unmistakably those of giants.

The entire village of Northeast was aroused by the discovery and today hundreds of people from this city took advantage of their holiday to visit the scene. It was first conjectured that the remains were those of soldiers killed in battle with the Indians that abounded in the vicinity during the last century, but the size of the skulls and the length of the leg bones dispelled that theory. So far about 150 giant skeletons of powerful proportions have been exhumed and indications point to a second cave eastward, which may probably contain as many more. Scientists who have exhumed skeletons and made careful measurements of the bones say that they are the remains of a race of gigantic creatures, compared with which our tallest men would appear pygmies. There are no arrow-heads, stone hatchets, or other implements of war with the bodies. Some of the bones are on exhibition at the various stores. One is as thick as a good sized bucket.

THE NEW YORK TIMES, APRIL 5, 1886
MONSTER SKULLS AND BONES

CARTERSVILLE, Ga., April 4.—The water has receded from the Tumlin Mound Field, and has left uncovered acres of skulls and bones. Some of these are gigantic. If the whole frame is in proportion to two thigh bones that were found, the owners must have stood 14 feet high. Many curious ornaments of shell, brass, and stone have been found. Some of the bodies were buried in small vaults built of stones. The whole makes a mine of archæological wealth. A representative of the Smithsonian Institution is here investigating the curious relics.

NEW YORK TIMES, FEBRUARY 11, 1902
NEW MEXICO DISCOVERY: 12-FOOT GIANT FOUND

Owing to the discovery of the remains of a race of giants in Guadalupe, New Mexico, antiquarians and archaeologists are preparing an expedition further to explore that region. This determination is based on the excitement that exists among the people of a scope of country near Mesa Rica, about 200 miles southeast of Las Vegas, where an old burial ground has been discovered that has yielded skeletons of enormous size. Luciana Quintana, on whose ranch the ancient burial plot is located, discovered two stones that bore curious inscriptions and beneath these were found in shallow excavations the bones of a frame that could not have been less than 12 feet in length. The men who opened the grave say the forearm was 4 feet long and that in a well-preserved jaw the lower teeth ranged from the size of a hickory nut to that of the largest walnut in size. The chest of the being is reported as having a circumference of seven feet. Quintana, who has uncovered many other burial places, expresses the opinion that perhaps thousands of skeletons of a race of giants long extinct, will be found. This supposition is based on the traditions handed down from the early Spanish invasion that have detailed knowledge of the existence of a race of giants that inhabited the plains of what now is Eastern New Mexico. Indian legends and carvings also in the same section indicate the existence of such a race.

NEW YORK TIMES, May 4, 1908
Cave in Mexico Gives up the Bones of Ancient Race

BOSTON, May 3- Charles C. Clapp, who has recently returned from Mexico, where he has been in charge of Thomas W. Lawson's mining interests, has called the attention of Prof. Agassiz to a remarkable discovery made by him.

He found in Mexico a cave containing some 200 skeletons of men each above eight feet in height. The cave was evidently the burial place of a race of giants who antedated the Aztecs. Mr. Clap arranged the bones of one of the skeletons and found the total length to be 8 feet 11 inches. The femur reached up to his thigh, and the molars were big enough to crack a cocoanut. The head measured eighteen inches from front to back.

MONROE COUNTY MAIL, JUNE 18, 1914
SCIENTISTS FIND GIANT SKELETON: IN LIFE THEY AVERAGED TWELVE FEET HIGH

Skeletons of a race of giants who averaged twelve feet in height were found by workmen engaged on a drainage project in Crowville, near here.

There are several score at least of the skeletons, and they lie in various positions. It is believed they were killed in a prehistoric fight and that the bodies lay where they fell until covered with alluvial deposits due to the flooding of the Mississippi River. No weapons of any sort were found at the site, and it is believed the Titans must have struggled with wooden clubs. The skulls are in a perfect state of preservation, and some of the jawbones are large enough to surround a baby's body.

Although the internet provides access to an abundance of photographs of skeletal remains of giants ranging from 10 to 15 feet in height (and larger) unearthed in the middle east, Europe, and even the United States from the Neolithic time period, none of these were included due to the possibility of fraud and hoaxes with the advent of digital photography and the digital photo manipulation possible today.

The sheer number of discoveries of giants' remains documented from across North America and Europe demonstrates there is substantial archeological evidence of giants having existed.

Part 5
What Happened to the Giants?

Having considered how the giants originated, when and where they lived, and how large they were, let's next consider what happened to the various groups of giants mentioned in the Bible.

Chapter 5.1
What Happened to the Giants Before the Flood?

We have considered giants both before the Flood, and after the Flood from the days of Moses, Abraham, and David. The giants that lived before the Flood all perished prior to or with the coming of the Flood.

> I Peter 3:20
> Which sometime were disobedient, when once the longsuffering of God waited in the days of Noah, while the ark was a preparing, wherein few, that is, eight souls were saved by water.

Only eight people survived the Flood: Noah, his wife, his three sons, and their wives. Everyone else perished with the Flood, including the giants.

Chapter 5.2
What Happened to the Giants in the Days of Moses?

The Anakims

From the time of Moses, we first considered the giants that
the spies encountered when they entered into the Promised
Land to spy it out.

> Numbers 13:22
> And they [the spies sent out by Moses] ascended by
> the south, and came unto Hebron; where Ahiman,
> Sheshai, and Talmai, the children of Anak, *were.*

These giants continued to live in the same area for the next
forty years until the children of Israel came into the land to
possess it. Of the 12 spies who originally entered into the
land to spy it out, only two remained when they entered
into the Promised Land: Joshua and Caleb. It is quite fitting
that these two men were involved with these three giants
once again over 40 years later, since they were the only two
out of the 12 spies unafraid to enter the land, and are
recorded as saying Numbers 14:9, "...neither fear ye the
people of the land; for they are bread for us: their defence is
departed from them, and the LORD is with us: fear them
not."

> Joshua 15:13-14
> And unto Caleb the son of Jephunneh he gave a part
> among the children of Judah, according to the
> commandment of the LORD to Joshua, *even* the

city of Arba the father of Anak, which *city is* Hebron.

And Caleb drove thence the three sons of Anak, Sheshai, and Ahiman, and Talmai, the children of Anak.

Caleb is recorded as driving the sons of Anak—Sheshai, Ahiman, and Talmai—out of Hebron, the land he was given as a possession. The Book of Judges provides us with more information about what ultimately happened to these three giants.

Judges 1:9-10
And afterward the children of Judah went down to fight against the Canaanites, that dwelt in the mountain, and in the south, and in the valley.

And Judah went against the Canaanites that dwelt in Hebron: (now the name of Hebron before *was* Kirjatharba:) and they slew Sheshai, and Ahiman, and Talmai.

Although Joshua 15:14 informs us that Caleb drove the three sons of Anak (Sheshai, Ahiman, and Talmai) out of Hebron, Judges 1:10 further informs us that they were slain also. As for the rest of the tribe of the Anakims in the land of Israel, Joshua destroyed them.

Joshua 11:21-22
And at that time came Joshua, and cut off the Anakims from the mountains, from Hebron, from

Debir, from Anab, and from all the mountains of Judah, and from all the mountains of Israel: Joshua destroyed them utterly with their cities.

There was none of the Anakims left in the land of the children of Israel: only in Gaza, in Gath, and in Ashdod, there remained.

In addition to Sheshai, Ahiman, and Talmai, there were other Anakims living in Debir, Anab, and in the mountains of Judah and Israel. Caleb drove the Anakims out of Hebron and Joshua cut them off from the mountains and destroyed them along with all of the other Anakims living in Debir, Anab, and the mountains of Judah and Israel. They were completely destroyed along with their cities. The only Anakims left were in Gaza, Gath, and Ashdod, cities of the Canaanites.

Og the King of Bashan

We have also considered one other giant from the time of Moses: Og the king of Bashan.

Deuteronomy 3:1-7
Then we turned, and went up the way to Bashan: and Og the king of Bashan came out against us, he and all his people, to battle at Edrei.

And the LORD said unto me, Fear him not: for I will deliver him, and all his people, and his land, into thy hand; and thou shalt do unto him as thou didst unto Sihon king of the Amorites, which dwelt at Heshbon.

So the LORD our God delivered into our hands Og also, the king of Bashan, and all his people: and we smote him until none was left to him remaining.

And we took all his cities at that time, there was not a city which we took not from them, threescore cities, all the region of Argob, the kingdom of Og in Bashan.

All these cities *were* fenced with high walls, gates, and bars; beside unwalled towns a great many.

And we utterly destroyed them, as we did unto Sihon king of Heshbon, utterly destroying the men, women, and children, of every city.

But all the cattle, and the spoil of the cities, we took for a prey to ourselves.

Og and all of the men, women, and children of Bashan were utterly destroyed. The children of Israel took all of his cities, which totaled 60 fenced cities with high walls and gates, and un-walled towns that were "a great many" in number. They also took all of the cattle and spoil of the cities for themselves.

Deuteronomy 3:11
For only Og king of Bashan remained of the remnant of giants [*rephaim*]; behold, his bedstead *was* a bedstead of iron; *is* it not in Rabbath of the

children of Ammon? nine cubits *was* the length thereof, and four cubits the breadth of it, after the cubit of a man.

It is also significant that Og was the very last remnant of the tribe of the giants known as the Rephaim. When he was killed, the entire tribe of the Rephaim ceased to exist.

Chapter 5.3
What Happened to the Giants in the Days of Abraham?

We have considered the giants who lived before the Flood and what happened to them. We have also considered what happened to the giants that lived in the time of Moses. Next, we will consider what happened to the giants who lived during the time of Abraham. We read about at least three tribes of giants in Genesis 14.

> Genesis 14:5-6
> And in the fourteenth year came Chedorlaomer, and the kings that *were* with him, and smote the Rephaims in Ashteroth Karnaim, and the Zuzims in Ham, and the Emims in Shaveh Kiriathaim.
>
> And the Horites in their mount Seir, unto Elparan, which *is* by the wilderness.

As the four kings from the Mesopotamian region journeyed first northwest from Mesopotamia then southward toward the southern end of the Salt Sea, they first destroyed the Rephaims in Ashteroth Karnaim, then farther south the Zuzims/Zamzummims in Ham, next the Emims in Shaveh Kiriathaim, and finally the Horims in Mount Seir.

The Rephaims were the tribe of giants of which Og was the last remnant in the days of Moses. They lived in the same area and town as Og in Ashteroth Karnaim. They were the first tribe destroyed by the four kings in the days of Abraham.

The next two groups of giants mentioned in Genesis 14:5 are the Zuzims and the Emims. Their history was described by Moses to the children of Israel as they were journeying around the southeastern side of the Salt Sea, or the Dead Sea, on their way to the Promised Land.

> Deuteronomy 2:9-11
> And the LORD said unto me, Distress not the Moabites, neither contend with them in battle: for I will not give thee of their land *for* a possession; because I have given Ar unto the children of Lot *for* a possession.
>
> The Emims dwelt therein in times past, a people great, and many, and tall, as the Anakims;
>
> Which also were accounted giants, as the Anakims; but the Moabites call them Emims.
>
> Deuteronomy 2:19-21
> And *when* thou comest nigh over against the children of Ammon, distress them not, nor meddle with them: for I will not give thee of the land of the children of Ammon *any* possession; because I have given it unto the children of Lot *for* a possession.
>
> (That also was accounted a land of giants: giants dwelt therein in old time; and the Ammonites call them Zamzummims;
>
> A people great, and many, and tall, as the Anakims; but the LORD destroyed them before them; and they succeeded them, and dwelt in their stead:

Although the record from Deuteronomy 2:20 and following says the Zamzummims and the Horites were destroyed by the Lord, it does not state how or by what means they were destroyed. As we have seen and understand from reading the record in Genesis chapter 14, the Rephaims, the Zuzims/Zamzummims, the Emims, and the Horites/Horims were all destroyed by the armies of the four kings from the Mesopotamian area as they moved southward to battle the five kings from the cities of the plain. Where Deuteronomy 2:20 and following says they were destroyed by the Lord, it would therefore allow one to conclude the means by which the Lord destroyed these tribes was by the four kings from the Mesopotamian area.

Chapter 5.4
What Happened to the Giants in the Days of David?

We have already considered what happened to the giants who lived before the Flood, the giants who lived in the time of Moses, and the giants who lived in the days of Abraham. Lastly, we will consider what happened to the giants that lived during the time of David.

Previously, when we considered the giants encountered by Caleb and Joshua, it was said that they rid the Promised Land of all giants completely—the only Anakims left at that time were said to live in Gaza, Gath, and Ashdod, cities of the Canaanites.

> Joshua 11:22
> There was none of the Anakims left in the land of the children of Israel: only in Gaza, in Gath, and in Ashdod, there remained.

Later, during the days of David, this land was also known as the land of the Philistines. This is where David and his men encountered giants. The first giant encountered by David was Goliath of Gath when David was a young man. Dr. Bullinger in the *Companion Bible* states David was 16 or 17 years of age at the time.[45]

---

[45] *The Companion Bible,* page 438, note on verse II Samuel 21:15

I Samuel 17:4
And there went out a champion out of the camp of the Philistines, named Goliath, of Gath, whose height *was* six cubits and a span.

As previously discussed, Goliath would have been approximately 9 feet 9 inches tall and was armed with the best armor and weapons available for that day and time. To many, he would have appeared to have been the ultimate weapon and an insurmountable force.

Of all the giants spoken of in God's Word, it is most interesting that the only words recorded spoken by a giant are those of Goliath. What he is recorded as saying is also equally interesting to consider.

I Samuel 17:8-11
And he stood and cried unto the armies of Israel, and said unto them, Why are ye come out to set *your* battle in array? *am* not I a Philistine, and ye servants to Saul? choose you a man for you, and let him come down to me.

If he be able to fight with me, and to kill me, then will we be your servants: but if I prevail against him, and kill him, then shall ye be our servants, and serve us.

And the Philistine said, I defy the armies of Israel this day; give me a man, that we may fight together.

When Saul and all Israel heard those words of the Philistine, they were dismayed, and greatly afraid.

I Samuel 17:16
And the Philistine drew near morning and evening, and presented himself forty days.

This challenge of Goliath continued every morning and evening for 40 days. As a result of Goliath's words, Saul and all of the army of Israel were discouraged and greatly afraid. Earlier, we discussed the meaning of the Hebrew word *nephil* from Numbers 13:33 when considering the giants from both before and after the Flood. We saw *Strong's Exhaustive Concordance of the Bible* define the word *nephil* in part as a "bully or tyrant." The words and actions of Goliath would certainly fit with this definition.

I Samuel 17:22-26
And David left his carriage in the hand of the keeper of the carriage, and ran into the army, and came and saluted his brethren.

And as he talked with them, behold, there came up the champion, the Philistine of Gath, Goliath by name, out of the armies of the Philistines, and spake according to the same words: and David heard *them.*

And all the men of Israel, when they saw the man, fled from him, and were sore afraid.

And the men of Israel said, Have ye seen this man that is come up? surely to defy Israel is he come up: and it shall be, *that* the man who killeth him, the king will enrich him with great riches, and will give

him his daughter, and make his father's house free
in Israel.

And David spake to the men that stood by him,
saying, What shall be done to the man that killeth
this Philistine, and taketh away the reproach from
Israel? for who *is* this uncircumcised Philistine, that
he should defy the armies of the living God?

Apparently, only David recognized the spiritual reality that
this "uncircumcised Philistine," in defying the armies of the
living God, was in fact defying God Himself. If he was not
the only one, he was certainly the only one present who
was courageous and bold enough to state the spiritual
reality of this confrontation and affront by Goliath.[46]

I Samuel 17:32
And David said to Saul, Let no man's heart fail
because of him; thy servant will go and fight with
this Philistine.

Only David, a 16 or 17 year old shepherd, was unafraid to
meet the challenge of Goliath.

I Samuel 17:40-45
And he took his staff in his hand, and chose him
five smooth stones out of the brook, and put them in
a shepherd's bag which he had, even in a scrip; and

---

[46] David is recorded receiving the spirit of God upon him "from that
day forward" when he was anointed by Samuel in I Samuel 16:13. This
should not be ignored in understanding the decisions and actions he
took for God against Goliath.

his sling *was* in his hand: and he drew near to the Philistine.

And the Philistine came on and drew near unto David; and the man that bare the shield *went* before him.

And when the Philistine looked about, and saw David, he disdained him: for he was *but* a youth, and ruddy, and of a fair countenance.

And the Philistine said unto David, *Am* I a dog, that thou comest to me with staves? And the Philistine cursed David by his gods.

And the Philistine said to David, Come to me, and I will give thy flesh unto the fowls of the air, and to the beasts of the field.

Then said David to the Philistine, Thou comest to me with a sword, and with a spear, and with a shield: but I come to thee in the name of the LORD of hosts, the God of the armies of Israel, whom thou hast defied.

Even in the face of Goliath's direct threats to David, he was the only one who was unafraid. He understood the true battle was not between Goliath and the army of Saul, but was between Goliath and God.

I Samuel 17:46-51
This day will the LORD deliver thee into mine hand; and I will smite thee, and take thine head

from thee; and I will give the carcases of the host of the Philistines this day unto the fowls of the air, and to the wild beasts of the earth; that all the earth may know that there is a God in Israel.

And all this assembly shall know that the LORD saveth not with sword and spear: for the battle *is* the LORD'S, and he will give you into our hands.

And it came to pass, when the Philistine arose, and came and drew nigh to meet David, that David hasted, and ran toward the army to meet the Philistine.

And David put his hand in his bag, and took thence a stone, and slang *it,* and smote the Philistine in his forehead, that the stone sunk into his forehead; and he fell upon his face to the earth.

So David prevailed over the Philistine with a sling and with a stone, and smote the Philistine, and slew him; but *there was* no sword in the hand of David.

Therefore David ran, and stood upon the Philistine, and took his sword, and drew it out of the sheath thereof, and slew him, and cut off his head therewith. And when the Philistines saw their champion was dead, they fled.

Thus, we have the record of what happened to the giant named Goliath.

Many years after this encounter with Goliath, David and his men again encountered more giants as they battled with the Philistines.

> II Samuel 21:15-17
>
> Moreover the Philistines had yet war again with Israel; and David went down, and his servants with him, and fought against the Philistines: and David waxed faint.
>
> And Ishbibenob, which *was* of the sons of the giant, the weight of whose spear *weighed* three hundred *shekels* of brass in weight, he being girded with a new *sword,* thought to have slain David.
>
> But Abishai the son of Zeruiah succoured him, and smote the Philistine, and killed him. Then the men of David sware unto him, saying, Thou shalt go no more out with us to battle, that thou quench not the light of Israel.

On this occasion, as David and his men battled with the army of the Philistines, another giant named Ishbibenob watched King David from afar. As David grew faint, exhausted from battle, Ishbibenob, who was armed with a new sword, thought to take advantage of the fatigued king and kill him. But Abishai, one of David's three primary captains, came to David's aid and killed the giant.

After this occasion, there were still more giants encountered in battle by David and company.

II Samuel 21:18-22

And it came to pass after this, that there was again a battle with the Philistines at Gob: then Sibbechai the Hushathite slew Saph, which *was* of the sons of the giant.

And there was again a battle in Gob with the Philistines, where Elhanan the son of Jaareoregim, a Bethlehemite, slew *the brother of* Goliath the Gittite, the staff of whose spear *was* like a weaver's beam.

And there was yet a battle in Gath, where was a man of *great* stature, that had on every hand six fingers, and on every foot six toes, four and twenty in number; and he also was born to the giant.

And when he defied Israel, Jonathan the son of Shimea the brother of David slew him.

These four were born to the giant in Gath, and fell by the hand of David, and by the hand of his servants.

There were a total of five giants killed either by David or his men. Goliath is recorded in I Samuel 17, and the other four are spoken of in II Samuel 21, verses 18-22. II Samuel 21:22 declares that these four were born to the giant in Gath, who is unnamed. In verse 19, one was described as being *"the brother of* Goliath." The words *"the brother of"* being in italics points out that these words were added by the translators to help in ease of reading. It is possible he could have been the son of Goliath. However, with the giant from Gath never being identified, the exact family relationship is uncertain. One thing is certain—the factor of family genetics cannot be ignored in the production of the giants recorded in the Bible.

Part 6
Summary and Conclusion

What about giants in the Bible?

Although largely overlooked and ignored, we have seen that the Bible declares that there were giants on the earth throughout much of human history, both before and after the Flood.

While the lineage of giants before the Flood was destroyed with its coming, after the Flood giants once again appeared rather quickly and are recorded living in at least four different areas of the Bible lands. All appear to have originated from their own families and tribes. They also appear to have been the original possessors of the lands in which they each dwelled after the Flood.

Abraham was born in the ninth generation after the Flood. He was born less than 300 years after it occurred. By the days of Abraham the number of giants had grown beyond families and tribes. From biblical records, one can see the areas they inhabited and, by definition, they should be considered an entire race.

The incorrect speculation that the giants of biblical record were the result of spirit beings mating with human females has caused difficulty for some. The giants, both before and after the Flood, did not originate by angels mating with human females. The phrase "sons of God" referred to in

107

Genesis 6:2 and 4 is a Hebraism, a type of figure of speech, which refers to men that followed after God, believed Him, and did His Will rather than followed after their own desires. They are placed in opposition to the "daughters of men" who did not follow after God.

The giants recorded in the Bible were not feeble but were described as mighty men, bullies, tyrants, and men of war. They were clearly the result of a genetic strain, or strains. The science of genetics shows that when smaller groups only breed among themselves, various genetic characteristics arise very quickly. There are three occurrences of this happening early on in human history as recorded in the book of Genesis. This occurred with the children of Adam and Eve, the sons of Noah after the Flood, and after the language dispersion at Babel. These three events also account for the timing in which the giants appear in the Bible.

The Anakims were a tribe of giants that appear to have originated from the city of Kirjatharba, later known as Hebron. Hebron is documented as being an old city even by biblical standards. Anak was the son of Arba, of whom Kirjatharba, "the city of Arba," was named. The Anakims bore Anak's name and his distinguishing features. Centuries after Abraham, when Caleb and Joshua rid the land of giants, the Anakims, it was revealed they were not isolated to only one town or area. There were some living in Hebron, others scattered and living throughout the mountains of Judah and Israel, and also in the cities of Debir and Anab. After all the Anakims were removed from the Promised Land, there were still some that remained in the cities of Gaza, Gath, and Ashdod. Hundreds of years later, King David encountered what would appear to have been remnants of these giants from the Philistine city of Gath.

The Rephaims lived in an area northeast to southeast of the Sea of Chinnereth (the Sea of Galilee) in the town and area of Ashtaroth. The Zamzummims, also known of as the Zuzims, lived to the south of the Rephaims in the land later occupied by the Ammorites. The Emims lived further south in the land later occupied by the Moabites, east of the Salt Sea. In the case of the Anakims, Rephaims, Zamzummims, and the Emims, it appears they were the first occupants of those lands after the Flood as there are no biblical records of any inhabitants living in those areas prior to their occupying them. It is quite possible there were other tribes of giants living south and southwest of the Salt Sea also. However, there are no other verses that can corroborate that any of those tribes were in fact giants as well.

As to how large the giants in the Bible were, there are both biblical descriptions and archeological evidence. Although there are only two specific references describing the size of the giants—Goliath standing approximately 10 feet tall and Og's bed that measured approximately 13 feet 6 inches long by 6 feet wide—both of these biblical descriptions agree with modern archeological evidence of giants. Combining biblical evidence and modern day archeological evidence, the size of the giants varies from approximately 8 to 15 feet in height. This certainly adds insight to the description by the spies sent out by Moses as they returned and related, "We were in our own sight as grasshoppers, and so we were in their sight."

The archeological evidence also supports there having been a race of giants living on the earth both before and after the Flood. Their remains have been dated by archeologists to be from what is known as the Neolithic period, ranging from the dawn of modern man up through 2,000 B.C.

As to what happened to the giants of record in the Bible, very simply, they were all destroyed. The giants who lived prior to the Flood either died before the Flood or at its coming. Three of the four tribes of giants considered—the Rephaims, the Emims, and the Zamzummims, who lived after the Flood in the days of Abraham—are recorded as being destroyed by the four kings from the Mesopotamian area in Genesis chapter 14. Og, the King of Bashan, the last remaining remnant of the Rephaims, was killed by Moses and the children of Israel as he came out against them in battle. The Anakims living in Hebron, the hill country of Judah, Israel, and the cities of Debir and Anab were either killed or driven out of the land by Caleb and Joshua. There were Anakims said to still be living at that time in the cities of Gaza, Gath, and Ashdod. Since they were not relevant to the Old Testament record of Israel, their history and demise is not recorded. However, hundreds of years later in the days of King David there were five giants recorded as being from Gath, and they were all killed by David or his men.

It is most interesting that giants are so prevalent in the folklore and mythology of so many countries and lands. It is also interesting, but not surprising, to find that there is a substantial history of them recorded in the Bible.

When one reads of there being giants in the Bible, one should understand that these are not fables or exaggerations of isolated incidents. These accounts are historically true as II Peter 1:20 and 21 exhort all to know and understand: "Knowing this first, that no prophecy of the scripture is of any private interpretation. For the prophecy came not in old time by the will of man: but holy men of God spake as they were moved by the Holy Ghost [Holy Spirit, meaning God]." God is the Author of the Bible, and He had many writers who spoke and wrote on His behalf. The biblical records looked at and considered herein were not given and did not come by the will of man. These are true historical records.

Appendix 1
Map of the Bible Lands
For the Times of Abraham Through Moses

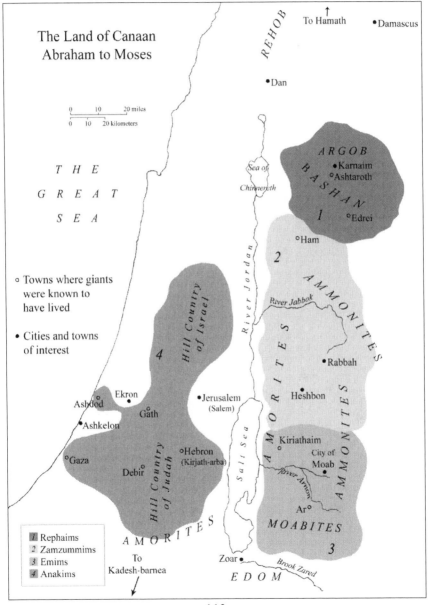

Appendix 2
Size Comparison Chart

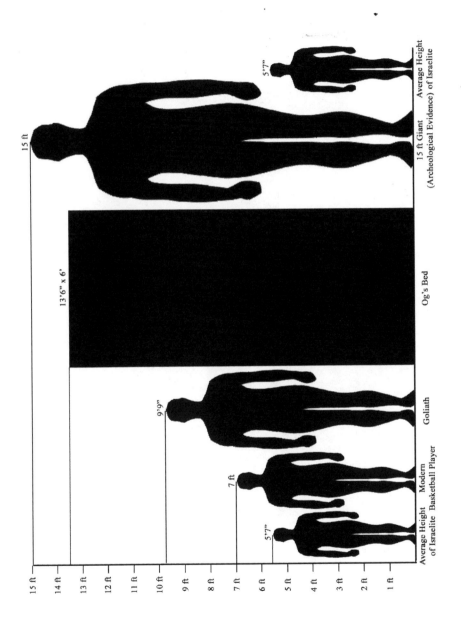

Appendix 3
The Conception of Jesus Christ

In our consideration of giants in the Bible, we have seen that spirit beings cannot reproduce with flesh and blood. This may raise questions regarding the conception of Jesus Christ and how God, Who is Spirit, could produce a son with Mary.

Toward the conclusion of the fall of man as recorded in Genesis chapter 3, God made a promise to the serpent, the devil.

> Genesis 3:15
> And I will put enmity between thee and the woman, and between thy seed and her seed; it shall bruise thy head, and thou shalt bruise his heel.

This verse contains the first reference to Jesus Christ in the Bible, as he is referred to here as "her seed," referring to the seed of the woman. God promised to put enmity, hostility, between the devil and the woman, and between the seed of the devil and the woman's seed. Speaking of the seed of the woman, God told the devil it would bruise his head and that he, the devil, would bruise the seed of the woman's heel.

In addressing this monumental statement by God to the devil, Dr. E. W. Bullinger wrote in Appendix 19 of *The Companion Bible* the following: "When it is said in verse 15 'thou shalt bruise his heel,' it cannot mean his literal heel of flesh and blood, but suffering, more temporary in character. When it said 'He shall crush thy head,' it means something more than a skull of bone, and brain, and hair. It means that all of Satan's plans and plots, policy and purposes, will one day be finally crushed and ended, never more to mar or to hinder the purposes of God."

An offspring of the woman was promised who will ultimately destroy God's adversary and his works. This is the first of many promises of an individual to come who would redeem mankind from his fallen state and defeat God's adversary, the devil.

What also arrests one's attention in Genesis 3:15 is the description of the woman's offspring as "her seed." What makes this statement so unusual is that seed does not originate with the female of the species, but from the male side. Although Genesis 3:15 does not offer an explanation about who the donor of the seed would be, it certainly calls attention to its importance by the manner in which it is stated.

In every conception there are two necessary elements: the egg and the sperm. The sperm is also referred to biblically as the seed. The egg is supplied by the female and the sperm, or seed, is supplied by the male.

Part of Jesus Christ's genetic makeup came from his mother, Mary. The male side, the seed, was contributed by God.

God did indeed intervene into the affairs of mankind in order to bring about the promised seed of Genesis 3:15, the savior and redeemer of mankind, Jesus Christ. But God did not cohabit or have sexual intercourse with Mary, nor did He violate her freedom of will.

> Luke 1:26-38
> And in the sixth month the angel Gabriel was sent from God unto a city of Galilee, named Nazareth,
>
> To a virgin espoused to a man whose name was Joseph, of the house of David; and the virgin's name *was* Mary.
>
> And the angel came in unto her, and said, Hail, *thou that art* highly favoured, the Lord *is* with thee: blessed *art* thou among women.
>
> And when she saw *him,* she was troubled at his saying, and cast in her mind what manner of salutation this should be.
>
> And the angel said unto her, Fear not, Mary: for thou hast found favour with God.
>
> And, behold, thou shalt conceive in thy womb, and bring forth a son, and shalt call his name JESUS.
>
> He shall be great, and shall be called the Son of the Highest: and the Lord God shall give unto him the throne of his father David:
>
> And he shall reign over the house of Jacob for ever; and of his kingdom there shall be no end.

Then said Mary unto the angel, How shall this be, seeing I know not a man?

And the angel answered and said unto her, The Holy Ghost shall come upon thee, and the power of the Highest shall overshadow thee: therefore also that holy thing which shall be born of thee shall be called the Son of God.

And, behold, thy cousin Elisabeth, she hath also conceived a son in her old age: and this is the sixth month with her, who was called barren.

For with God nothing shall be impossible.

And Mary said, Behold the handmaid of the Lord; be it unto me according to thy word. And the angel departed from her.

God sent the angel Gabriel, His messenger, to discuss His plan to produce the Messiah, the promised seed, with Mary. Mary agreed with His proposed plan as evidenced by her response to Gabriel in verse 38, "be it unto me according to thy word." God did not violate Mary's freedom of will. She believed Gabriel and agreed to be part of God's plan. God then created the sperm which fertilized the egg within a fallopian tube of Mary.[47]

---

[47] For more information, see *The Word's Way, Studies in Abundant Living Volume 111,* by Dr. Victor Paul Wierwille, The Conception of Jesus Christ, pages 157-174; *Jesus Christ Our Promised Seed,* by Dr. Victor Paul Wierwille, The Genealogy of Jesus Christ, pages 113-132.

The word "create" in the Bible is used exclusively of God; for only God can start with nothing and bring into existence something that previously did not exist. As we have seen and understand, God did not have sexual intercourse with Mary, as spirit cannot reproduce with flesh and blood, with soul life. This is not possible and would violate the foundational laws of genetics found in the first chapter of Genesis. Rather, God created the sperm which fertilized the egg within Mary. How ironically interesting it is that God created something so microscopically small, not even visible to the naked eye, which in turn changed the course of human history forever, thereby fulfilling the promise He made in Genesis 3:15.

Appendix 4
Articles from the NY Times Archives
November 21, 1856 – July 14, 1916

November 21, 1856	Skeleton of a Giant Found
October 3, 1862	A Race of Giants in Old Gaul
December 25, 1868	Discovery of A Hugh Skeleton
September 8, 1871	More Big Indians Found in Virginia
February 8, 1876	The Early American Giant
August 10, 1880	Two Very Tall Skeletons
May, 25, 1882	The Bones of a Giant Found
November 20, 1883	A Giant's Remains In A Mound
May 5, 1885	Skeletons 7 Feet Long
April 5, 1886	Monster Skulls And Bones
February 9, 1890	A Race of Indian Giants
August 10, 1891	The Wisconsin Mounds
March 5, 1894	Giants of Other Days
December 20, 1897	Wisconsin Mound Opened
February 11, 1902	New Mexico Discovery: 12 Foot Giant Found

To view a photo static copy of this article see:
http://query.nytimes.com/mem/archive-free/pdf?res=9B00E5DA1530E733A25752C1A9649C946397D6CF

September 7, 1904	Find Giant Indian Bones
May 4, 1908	Giants Skeletons Found
May 12, 1912	Strange Skeletons Found
July 14, 1916	Giant Bones In Mound

Additional articles from various newspapers may also be viewed at:

www.jasoncolavito.com/newspaper-accounts-of-giants.html

About the Author

Donnie Lamb has been involved with biblical research, teaching, and fellowship for over 40 years. He was ordained to the Christian ministry in August of 1983.

He has been married to his wife, Marcia, for over 41 years and they have three children, two sons-in-law, one daughter-in-law, and three grandchildren (with two more on the way).

Donnie and Marcia currently reside in Spokane, WA where he assists in pastoring a church and also does a weekly home fellowship along with his son and daughter-in-law. He drives a school bus for special needs students and after many years is finally working on getting his private pilot's license.

Donnie can be contacted at
whataboutgiantsinthebible@gmail.com.

Made in the USA
San Bernardino, CA
20 April 2017